Understanding Ethics

Understanding Ethics

An Introduction to Moral Theory

Second Edition

Torbjörn Tännsjö

Edinburgh University Press

© Torbjörn Tännsjö, 2002, 2008

Edinburgh University Press Ltd
22 George Square, Edinburgh

Reprinted 2009, 2010 (twice)

First edition published by
Edinburgh University Press in 2002

Typeset in Sabon
by Norman Tilley Graphics Ltd, and
printed and bound in Great Britain
by CPI Antony Rowe, Chippenham, Wilts

A CIP record for this book is available
from the British Library

ISBN 978 0 7486 3689 1 (hardback)
ISBN 978 0 7486 3690 7 (paperback)

Contents

Preface

This book is intended for anyone who wants to take up serious studies in normative ethics. In it I try to strike a reasonable balance between two goals. First of all, I give a short, clear and systematic statement of the most pressing normative problems facing humanity and their purported solutions. Second, I give some indication of where the articulation of the problems and their attempted solutions come from. The book can be used as a very elementary textbook. It gives an overview of the subject of normative ethics and it can be read by students with no previous experience at all of studies in philosophy. The book can stand on its own, but it can easily be combined with further literature covering part of, or all of, what is explored in the book. The book introduces the student to the subject of normative ethics as such but also to further reading.

This second edition is different from the first mainly in that it presents and discusses the so-called trolley cases, which everyone who takes up studies in moral philosophy is bound to encounter. They are described in Chapter 1, and are returned to in the successive chapters. It is indicated how the various different normative approaches try to cater for our intuitions with respect to these cases, and a discussion is also pursued, in the final chapter, about the normative relevance of recent findings in psychology and neuroscience concerning how people tend to think about them. This down-to-earth discussion in the final chapter of the methods of investigation actually used in the book has replaced a rather abstract discussion of such methods in the introductory chapter to the previous edition. Furthermore, many minor changes and clarifications have been made in order to render (even) easier the understanding of the arguments put forward in the book. The lists of suggested further reading have been thoroughly updated.

Practical and Normative Ethics

Practical problems

Anyone who, early in the twenty-first century, looks back over the last century in order to pass a moral judgement must become utterly sad. What we have left behind is a century preoccupied with terror, violence and injustice. This has brought the well-known British moral philosopher Jonathan Glover to make the following reflection:

> In Europe at the start of the twentieth century most people accepted the authority of morality. They thought there was a moral law, which was self-evidently to be obeyed. Immanuel Kant had written of the two things which fill the mind with admiration and awe, 'the starry heavens above me and the moral law within me'. In Cambridge in 1895, a century after Kant, Lord Acton still had no doubts: 'Opinions alter, manners change, creeds rise and fall, but the moral law is written on the tablets of eternity.' At the start of the twentieth century, reflective Europeans were also able to believe in moral progress, and to see human viciousness and barbarism as in retreat. At the end of the century, it is hard to be confident either about the moral law or about moral progress. (*Humanity*, p. 1)

A striking fact, when the recent past is contemplated, is that not only have many political leaders and powerful men, together with their close collaborators, committed crimes and outright atrocities against humanity, but also, and even more disturbingly, that so many 'ordinary' people have allowed them to do so. One gets the impression that ordinary, decent people, in their relation to the atrocities of their time, must have been suffering from moral blindness. When they were not themselves among the victims, they allowed all sorts of evil to be perpetrated. It is as if they had never been aware of the existence of any moral law. Or did they hold values so different from the ones we would like to think we hold today that they mistook crime for justice?

It is hard to tell whether they were ignorant or just had a different mindset from ours. It is easy, however, to pass moral judgements on the past. But what about our present age? One burning question for us is the following. Are there practices in advanced, industrialised and 'civilised' societies that are just as evil as the practices of the past that we do not hesitate today to call crimes? Do we too perform acts or sustain practices that future generations will refer to as atrocities?

I am not the first person to raise this question. Three areas have often been cited as examples of how terrible things are allowed to go on relatively unnoticed: (1) our (the human species') repression of other species (animals); (2) our (all human beings') complacency in our relation to the destruction of our environment, global warming being the most well-known and discussed example; and (3) our (the rich part of the world's) tolerance of famine and abject poverty in the poor parts of the world. I will return many times in this book to these three themes. For the moment, let me use just one of them as an example. I shall focus on the relation between us (people like you who read this and me, the writer) and people living in abject poverty in poor parts of the world in order to introduce the subject of this book. I who write this and you who read it are, I assume, relatively well-off, living in a part of the world where abject poverty is rare. But we are not ignorant of the fact that things look very different elsewhere. On television almost every day we are shown children suffering from malnutrition, dying before our eyes from infectious diseases that are relatively trivial in our part of the world. Yet we do so little to help them. We 'tolerate' their suffering or 'blind' ourselves to it, just like people tolerated or blinded themselves when others were enslaved two centuries ago, or when people were systematically discriminated against under the apartheid system in South Africa during the twentieth century. Does this mean that we are acting immorally?

Let me pose the problem as follows. Suppose we do our job or pursue our studies, that we care for those who are near and dear to us and pay our taxes (knowing that a small proportion is allocated to international aid). Does all this mean that we are obeying the moral law? Or are we violating it?

It is not my intention to answer a question like this one. Those who read this book will, however, be provided with better means to answer it for themselves. I now use the question as an example of what I call a 'practical' question. Characteristic of a practical question is that the answer to it is an action. My answer to the question posed is the way I decide to live my life. Your answer to it is the way you decide to live your life.

We always face practical questions, and the most basic practical question facing us all the time is what to do with the rest of our lives. But more restricted questions tend to crop up. Some of them seem almost as difficult as the grand question about what to do with the rest of our lives. A young woman becomes pregnant. Should she carry her pregnancy to term or seek an abortion? It turns out that she does not know who the father of her child is. Would it be right for her to seek prenatal tests in order to identify the father and then carry the pregnancy to term only if he is the 'right' man, but otherwise seek an abortion? Another woman knows that her mother and elder sister both suffer from breast cancer: would it be wise for her to try to find out through genetic testing whether she has the gene that predisposes her to the same disease? If she has the gene, would it be a good idea for her to have a double mastectomy, just to be sure she will not develop the disease? A young man has trained hard to become a top athlete. His doctor offers him a brand new, performance-enhancing drug, which is not on the list of prohibited (doping) substances, but which will most probably be listed once it becomes generally known. Would it be right for him to take advantage of his doctor's offer?

Practical problems need not be individual in nature. They often face us collectively and they sometimes take on a political slant. Here is a hard political practical problem: suppose we find out that there exists a certain gene, or complex of genes, that predisposes individuals to become 'psychopaths' or 'sociopaths'. Suppose we find out that, probably, those who were the most dedicated torturers in the concentration camps during the twentieth century had this gene. Suppose we find out that some of the most sadistic of today's murderers have it as well. And suppose a certain method of genetic therapy evolves which makes it possible to 'correct' this natural mistake. Should society tolerate the use of this kind of therapy? Should society make its use mandatory?

| (1) Moral principle |
| (2) Account of the relevant facts |
| (3) Practical conclusion |

Figure 1.1 Model for applied ethics

How do we solve practical problems? In particular, how do we solve them in a responsible manner? Here is a simplified answer to this question: we do applied ethics.

Applied ethics

The general idea behind applied ethics is the following: in order to gain knowledge about what to do in a practical situation we need true or reasonable moral principles to apply to the case under scrutiny. In order to be able to do this, we need also to get a grasp of the relevant facts of the situation. We then use the simple model set out in Figure 1.1

The statement of the moral principle (1) and the account of the relevant facts (2) render it possible to arrive at the practical conclusion (3). If the conclusion follows from the premises, we can say not only that we have an answer to the question of what to do, but also a kind of moral explanation of *why* this is what we ought to do.

Suppose we have found out that it would be right to tell a lie under certain circumstances. And suppose we have concluded that this would be right *because* telling this lie would be beneficial to the one to whom the lie is told. The fact that the lie is beneficial *explains* why it is right to tell it. Then we may also say that this characteristic of this lie is a 'right-making characteristic' of it. This characteristic is what *makes* the act right.

However, in life it is often very difficult to solve practical questions. Not only is it difficult to use the method just described; the method is also, as such, controversial. We will learn more about that in Chapters 6 and 7. Let us set these difficulties aside for the moment, however, and concentrate on the problems raised more immediately by the model. Let us examine them in relation to the practical problem already stated. Suppose I pay my taxes, care for those who are near and dear to me, apply myself to my studies or my work, but do nothing to help starving children living in poor parts of the world. Does this mean that I am acting immorally? Or would it be fair to say that I am obeying the moral law? In order to answer this question with the help of the model we must find true or reasonable moral principles to apply to the problem. Where do we find these principles? Let us hypothetically assume that we all have a moral duty to do whatever we can to make the world a decent place for everyone. What follows from this assumption? This depends on whether we can, in fact, contribute to the goal of making the world a decent place for everyone. One line of argument that could be put forward by someone who doubts this would be the following. By changing our way of life radically, each of us could do a lot to improve the situation in the world. We could give money to Oxfam, join organisations that supply medicine to those who really need it, become doctors ourselves and work in poor parts of the world, and so forth. By not changing our lives it could be said that we commit immoral acts. If we do not change the way that we live, we are perhaps no better than those who were living near the concentration camps during the last century, complacently watching the smoke rising from the chimneys of the crematorium furnaces while they went on performing string quartets and playing with their children.

But is this conclusion fair? One way of trying to rebut it would be as follows. It is certainly true that, to the extent that we can do something to rectify injustices in the world we should do so. But problems such as famine and abject poverty in foreign countries are much too difficult to solve to be the direct concern of any individual. Here only political means are effective. We ought to think carefully before we cast our vote in general elections, of course, in order to ensure that the political party with the best solution to these problems wins, but this is about as much as we can do.

Another way of trying to rebut the argument would be as follows. It may be true that, even if there is little I can do as an individual to eradicate poverty and famine in the world, there is something I can do to help individual people living in other parts of the world. But is this something I *have* to do if I want to be moral? Could it really be fair to say that unless I give up most of my belongings I am acting immorally? I do not think so. It is undeniable that if those who are poor and who suffer from disease and famine do so because I have wronged them, then I ought to compensate them. However, their misery is a result of natural causes or bad luck on their part, or at least not a result of any wrongdoing on my part. In which case it is fine if I help them, but from the point of view of morality, I may very well go on living the ordinary kind of life I do.

We have seen that in order to solve a practical problem we must have recourse to true or reasonable moral principles (a correct account of 'the moral law') and to an account of the relevant facts. And when we want to question the putative solution to a practical problem, we can question either the principles used to obtain the answer or the putative facts used in the same process. Note that which facts are relevant is determined by what practical question we want to answer and by what moral principle we take as our point of departure when we seek the solution. But what moral principle is the *true* or *reasonable* one? This is the question that will be discussed systematically in this book. And a systematic attempt to reach an answer to *this* question is made within what is often called 'normative ethics'.

Normative ethics can be seen as a subject in its own right, but in practice it cannot be pursued in isolation from applied ethics. How do we find true or reasonable moral principles? Well, one way of finding whether a suggested principle is true or reasonable is to apply it to a practical problem and see whether it yields a plausible solution. And it goes without saying that there is little point in mechanically 'applying' moral principles to practical questions without contemplating whether they are true or reasonable.

However, here we encounter another complication. It has turned out that in normative ethics it is often more convenient to discuss abstract thought-examples than real cases. Real cases are messy, they contain too much information to be possible to handle. In reality, everything *might* happen. Abstract thought-examples, on the other hand, can be devised so that we just *assume* that certain things are the case. The most famous example of this kind of reasoning is found in a series of thought-examples developed and elaborated upon by two philosophers, Philippa Foot and Judith Jarvis Thomson. I will return to them repeatedly in this book. In the original example, The Switch, a trolley is running down a track. In its path are five people who have been tied to the track. It is possible for you to flick a switch, which will divert the trolley down a different track. There is a single person tied to that track. Many believe that they should flick the switch. They argue that it is better to save five lives than to save one. However, others think it would be wrong to flick the switch. Is there a way for them to defend this decision? They may argue that it is always wrong actively to kill. If they do not flick the switch they do not kill actively, they merely allow five people to be killed.

However, here comes a variation of the example, The Footbridge. You are on a bridge under which a trolley will pass. There is a big man next to you and your only way to stop the trolley is to push him onto the track, killing him to save the five. Few think this would be right, even those who are prepared to flick the switch in the original example. Can they defend their decision? They can claim that it is wrong to intend the death of a person, as would be the case if they pushed the big man, but it is acceptable merely to foresee the death of a person, when death is not intended and when it means that more lives are saved, as in the original example.

Now, however, comes a third version of the example, The Loop. As in the first case, you can divert the trolley onto a separate track. On this track is a single big man. However, beyond the big man, the track loops back onto the main line towards the five, and if it weren't for the presence of the big man, flicking the switch would not save the five. Now many people, even people who hesitate to push the big man, agree to flick the switch.

How can they defend their decision? It seems that they are in trouble. Perhaps they have to go back and revise some of their earlier judgements. Or perhaps they can come up with some subtle difference between the two last cases. In any case, they have been drawn deeply into moral philosophical reasoning of the kind to be explored in this book.

One truth, many truths or no truth at all?

It might be thought that, from the very beginning, the search for one, unique, superior moral outlook ('the moral law') must be doomed, since there exists more than one such outlook. Moral truth may be thought to be relative. What from one cultural or temporal perspective is right may from another cultural or temporal perspective be wrong, it might be held. So there is no point in the pursuit of a uniquely superior moral outlook.

The threat from this kind of ethical relativism may seem real, but it should not be taken too seriously. In order to evaluate it, we must be more precise about its nature. Ethical relativism comes in many versions.

Ethical relativism is sometimes thought of as the view that each individual, culture or time is allowed to act in accordance with its own moral outlook. However, this is not 'relativism' in any interesting sense. This is one moral position among many others. The reader is invited to ponder whether ethical relativism can gain support from any of the basic outlooks discussed in this book, or whether it can serve as a superior alternative to all of them.

There is also a *semantic* version of moral relativism, the idea that when different people pass seemingly inconsistent moral judgements, they are not always actually contradicting each other, since each makes, in his or her moral judgement, an implicit reference to a certain system of rules. So when one person claims that slavery is all right, this means, upon closer inspection, that, according to the system of rules accepted in his society, slavery is acceptable, while when another person claims that slavery is wrong, this means that, according to the existing system of rules in her society, slavery is not acceptable.

I doubt that this view of our moral predicament is correct. However, even if it is, there is room for normative ethics. We still want to investigate what, from the point of view of a particular normative tradition (our own), is right and wrong and why it is right and wrong. Even moral relativists of this variety are usually prepared to engage in the pursuit of moral truth.

However, even if we need not worry that there is more than one moral truth to pursue, must we not still suspect that perhaps there is no such thing at all as moral truth? Could not moral nihilism be a threat to the very idea of normative ethics?

Some philosophers used to think that if moral beliefs are mere attitudes (what has been called 'emotivism'), and if there is no moral reality to which our moral beliefs could correspond or fail to correspond (what I will here call moral 'nihilism'), then there is no point in thinking hard about moral questions. This is not the place to discuss this matter at any length. Here it must suffice to note that nowadays few seem to share this kind of radical scepticism concerning normative ethics. It is generally claimed that even if there is no absolute truth to pursue in ethics, there is still a point in thinking through one's most basic moral ideas and to eliminate inconsistent arguments from one's moral thinking. To all who are prepared to do this, irrespective of whether they conceive of themselves as moral realists (believing that there is a unique moral truth to pursue in normative ethics) or moral nihilists (believing that, strictly speaking, there is no such thing as moral truth), this kind of book should be of help.

This is a book in normative ethics, not in metaethics, so I will not try to settle the dispute whether there is a unique moral truth to be found, or whether there are many or none at all. However, in the concluding chapter, where more is said about how we should conduct ourselves when pursuing normative ethics, I will make some comments on this matter. In particular, I will speculate about whether new scientific insights about how we come to hold the moral intuitions we do may shed light on the problem of truth in ethics.

Normative ethics

Before putting to one side the kind of semantic, epistemological and ontological questions just discussed (often called 'meta-ethical'), a brief remark should be made about the epistemic question cited above. How do we gain knowledge, or at least justified beliefs, about moral principles?

An easy answer would be to advocate the way the argument is conducted in this book. It is better to show than to tell how to go about it, in my opinion. However, let me give a very brief description of how I will go about it. We find some way of articulating bold moral conjectures such as these: It is always wrong deliberately and actively to kill an innocent human being. You should always act so as to maximise the sum total of welfare in the universe ... and so forth. We then apply them to real or hypothetical cases (in accordance with the model for applied ethics described above) and assess whether the conclusions we reach are acceptable. If several hypotheses are compatible with a particular judgement, we make an inference to the best explanation. The principle that gives the best explanation of *why* it is that you should act in a certain manner in a certain situation is the principle we give credence to. We then move on to other cases and find reasons to stick to our principle or to revise it. When the process has come to an end and we have reached what is often called a 'reflective equilibrium', we are entitled to conclude that we are justified in our moral beliefs.

Does this mean that our beliefs are also true or reasonable? It does not. In morality, just as in science, we are doomed to be fallible. Even an opinion that seems perfectly justified today may be rejected tomorrow.

In this book I will examine seven radically different, bold moral conjectures, each presenting a different idea about what is a sound point of departure when solving practical problems. Here is a list of them:

- utilitarianism (the idea that we ought always to act so as to maximise the sum total of welfare in the universe);
- egoism (the idea that we ought always to act so as to maximise the sum total of our own welfare);
- deontological ethics (according to which there are duties or prohibitions, binding upon the agent, irrespective of the consequences of following them);
- the ethics of rights (according to which each moral subject has certain rights that no one is entitled to violate, no matter how urgent this may seem);
- virtue ethics (according to which the most basic question in ethics is not what we ought to do, but what kind of persons we ought to be);
- feminist ethics (according to which women and men tend to think differently about moral and practical problems and according to which an assumed female way of thinking deserves particular attention);
- environmental or ecological ethics (according to which not only human beings and other sentient beings have moral status, but also nature itself; we have duties to preserve nature, irrespective of the consequences for sentient beings of doing so).

I will investigate what these moral theories amount to more precisely; I will test arguments for and against them, and consider their implications in various different fields. In relation to each of the theories, I will try to find the most plausible interpretation, but also its most troublesome implications.

The theories that are discussed are not only very different, they can also imply inconsistent answers to practical questions. It is not difficult, for example, to think of a situation where, according to utilitarianism, I ought to perform a certain action (it has the best consequences) while, at the same time, according to deontological ethics, this action is forbidden (it would mean deliberately killing an innocent human being). The existence of such conflicts renders it necessary to choose among the various different theories. Unless one modifies one's favoured moral principles when they conflict with each other, one will soon find that they offer no guidance at all. So, for practical reasons we have to make up our minds.

In addition to this practical reason for choosing among the theories, there seem to exist good intellectual reasons to make a choice among them as well, even if, in most situations, there is no obvious conflict. For unless we make a choice we will not know *why* we have the kinds of moral duties we have. Remember that a true or reasonable moral principle can explain why we ought to do such and such in a practical situation. And unless we have recourse to a *unique* principle, or at least a *consistent set* of principles, we have no explanation at all.

Suppose I find that I ought to send more money to starving children in poor countries and suppose I have found that this action is supported by both utilitarianism and a theory of moral rights, i.e. if I perform it, I both make the world a better place and compensate poor children for wrongs committed in the past by my ancestors. Then it may be obvious to me that I should send the money. However, I still want to know why this is so. Is it because by doing so I maximise the sum total of welfare, or is it to right a previous wrong? I may want to know the answer to this question out of mere intellectual curiosity, but I may also come to need it for practical reasons, when, some time in the future, I face a situation where these principles are in conflict (where I can maximise, say, the sum total of welfare only by violating a putative right).

It should be noted that the moral theories discussed in this book are formulated without any reference to God or religion.

What we today call virtue ethics was developed during antiquity, first and foremost by Aristotle some 300 years before Christ. Virtue ethics has had a renaissance since the 1960s. The other theories were first articulated in modern times (if we assume that modernity dates from the sixteenth century). Egoism, in its most attractive version, was presented by the English philosopher Thomas Hobbes (1588–1679). The most well-known advocate of deontological ethics was the great German philosopher Immanuel Kant (1724–1804). The theory of moral rights was articulated by the English philosopher John Locke (1632–1704). Utilitarianism was defended by another English philosopher and great social reformer, Jeremy Bentham (1748–1832). The feminist approach to ethics was recently developed by philosophers who took their point of departure in empirical studies of the moral development of girls and boys conducted by the American developmental psychologist Carol Gilligan. Even the environmental (or ecological) approach to ethics was articulated quite recently; two of the pioneers are the American thinker Aldo Leopold, who created what he called a 'Land Ethic', and the Norwegian philosopher Arne Naess, who coined the term 'deep ecology' (to be explained in due course).

Even if some of these philosophers believed in God, or could be said to be religious, God, or religion, plays little or no role in their moral philosophies. Is this a mere coincidence? I think not. Even if God exists, he cannot come to the rescue when we want to settle practical or moral problems. Let me briefly explain why.

Religion and morality

In the public discussion of practical or moral problems, representatives of the various different religions often take a leading role. And these religious leaders make great claims. In sometimes rather pompous terms they assert that what they represent are moral outlooks based on their respective religions, outlooks such as Christian, Jewish or Muslim ethics. In a way they are right. The moral outlooks they represent are actually held by many people adhering to the respective religions. Often there are also certain authoritative documents stating exactly what moral outlooks are required by the adherents of these religions. It may therefore be a good idea to include representatives of the most important religions in governmental committees preparing controversial laws on gene therapy, the cloning of embryos, euthanasia, and so forth. However, the fact that people who are united by their religious beliefs tend also to be united by their moral beliefs does not mean that there is any essential connection between religion and morality. In particular, nothing of what has been said implies that religion (a belief in God) is necessary, or even of any help, to those who want to form a consistent and reasonable moral outlook.

Are there any such connections between religion and morality? Is it true, for example, as the Russian author Fyodor Dostoyevsky used to claim, that if God is dead, then everything is permitted?

Dostoyevsky was mistaken. No moral conclusion whatever follows from the assumption that God does, or does not, exist (and the conclusion that everything is permitted is indeed a moral conclusion). Let us see in more detail why no moral conclusion follows from the assumption that God exists.

In general, three lines of argument exist, intended to support the view that God is required in morality. (1) Some thinkers have claimed that if God exists, then it is up to him to decide about what is right and wrong. (2) Other thinkers have made the more modest claim that even if God cannot decide about right and wrong, he can show us the right way. (3) Finally, there are those who have claimed that even if God cannot decide about right or wrong, or show us the right way, he can at least give us a good reason to behave morally. We should accept none of this.

The medieval English philosopher William of Ockham (1285–1349) exemplifies the first position. According to Ockham, God is free to determine for human beings what they should do. What God wills us to do determines what is right for us to do. Disobedience to God's will defines sin. But this is not a plausible view. First of all, can a decision by any agent really make an action right? That is, can we explain why we ought not to kill with reference to the putative fact that this accords with God's will? This does not strike me as a plausible candidate for making an action right. Second, and even more importantly, if God could determine what is right and wrong, that is, if God's will made an action right, then this would mean that had God willed us to murder, then murder would have been right. But this is absurd. Even from a theological point of view this must be hard to believe. Moreover, we are used to thinking of God as almighty, omniscient and infinitely good. But with this notion God's infinite goodness turns into something close to conceit.

But even if God cannot decide about right or wrong, can he not at least guide us in our practical choices? This was the opinion of another famous medieval thinker, the Italian philosopher Thomas Aquinas (1225–74). According to Aquinas, God is good, not because he decides about good and evil, but because he cannot help willing what is good. His actions can no more be at variance with the moral law than with the laws of logic. But does not this mean that God can at least instruct us about what to do? He can teach us about right and wrong actions. Even this position is problematic, however.

First of all, even if God can tell us what to do, we want to know *why* we ought to do it as well. To realise this takes independent moral *reflection* on our side.

Second, *is* it really possible for God to inform us about right and wrong actions? Suppose he wants to tell us that we should not kill each other. Now, even if he does send us this message, how do we *know* that this information originates from God (an infinitely good being) and not from Satan? Even if we find the message in the Holy Scripture, or if it is communicated to us by the Pope speaking on behalf of Almighty God, we might suspect that the message comes from Satan rather than from God. Yes, even if we hear the message shouted at us from an old man with a white beard looking down at us from the sky, we must suspect that he may be an impostor. There is only one way for us to ascertain that the message is genuine: by comparing it with what we have independently come to believe is the moral truth. But that means the advice from God has not reached us until it is too late. We already know what he wants to tell us.

But if God can neither decide about right or wrong actions, nor give us moral advice, can he not at least provide us with a good reason to do what is right?

This is, of course, the form that the reference to religion in the moral education of people has most often taken. Representatives of religious and political authorities have instructed their followers to abide by various different moral codes and they have promised those who do that they will be richly compensated by eternal bliss, while those who do not have been threatened that, in order to redeem their sins, they will have to experience eternal torture in Hell. It would be foolhardy to deny that these injunctions have been effective. However, it should be noted that what is achieved is selfish rather than genuinely moral behaviour. By reference to how God is prepared to treat them, people are persuaded to do the right thing – but for the wrong (egoistic) reason.

The structure of the book

In what follows I describe and discuss seven moral theories: utilitarianism, egoism, deontological ethics, the ethics of rights, virtue ethics, feminist ethics and environmental or ecological ethics. I will try to find 'pure' versions of each theory, that is, I will avoid mixing them with each other and I will try to find their most plausible versions. I then go on to discover the most troublesome aspects of each.

The reason that I start with utilitarianism is not that utilitarianism is the oldest or most respected moral theory. Rather, it is the most extensively discussed theory, and also the theory that is most sophisticated in the sense that all sorts of answers have been devised to counter critical points raised against it. It is also true that the other theories are often put forward in recent discussions as attempts to account for what have been considered to be the *failures* of utilitarianism. So, a discussion of the putative *failures* of utilitarianism naturally leads on to the other theories.

Note that the fact that utilitarianism is a highly sophisticated and elaborate view can in no way be taken to show that it is also a very plausible view. It is an open question whether sophistication and elaboration in morality really lead to truth. Indeed, one of the controversies in normative ethics concerns this very fact. So it does not automatically count in utilitarianism's favour that it is sophisticated and elaborate. Some have even held that this counts against it. Be that as it may, utilitarianism is, for strictly pedagogical reasons, a perfect place to start the journey that will carry us through the seven moral theories selected for examination.

Are there any other theories that we should have discussed as well? Although it may seem rash to say so, I think not! The ones selected for consideration are, as far as it is possible to tell today, the most plausible candidates for a true or reasonable moral theory. However, it may be that some combination of them is what some of us will tend to believe is the closest to moral truth that we can achieve. I will comment briefly on the possibility of a mixed theory at the end of our journey. But the time has now come to embark on it.

Suggested introductory reading on ethics

The quotation from Jonathan Glover is from *Humanity: A Moral History of the Twentieth Century* (London: Jonathan Cape, 1999), p. 1. The trolley example was first formulated by Philippa Foot in 'The Problem of Abortion and the Doctrine of the Double Effect', *Oxford Review*, 1967, and is reproduced in her book *Virtues and Vices* (Oxford: Oxford University Press, 1978). Judith Jarvis Thomson elaborates on the example in 'Killing, Letting Die, and the Trolley Problem', *The Monist*, 1967. Those who want to get to know recent influential philosophers engaged in normative ethics should consult T. Petersen and J. Ryberg (eds), *Normative Ethics: 5 Questions* (Automatic Press/VIP, 2007); here normative ethicists describe how they conceive of their subject and how they were originally drawn to it. There are several introductory texts to normative ethics, although most of them contain metaethical material as well. Two classic introductions, defending definite answers to normative problems, are Peter Singer's *Practical Ethics*, 2nd edition (Cambridge: Cambridge University Press, 1993) and Jonathan Glover's *Causing Death and Saving Lives* (Harmondsworth: Penguin, 1977). Shelly Kagan has written a highly instructive but difficult introduction, *Normative Ethics* (Boulder, CO: Westview Press, 1998). Electronic media are extremely helpful when a reader wants to pursue a particular question further. In particular I recommend the *Stanford Encyclopedia of Philosophy*, which is free for everyone to access: http://plato.stanford.edu/entries/rights/. There are several anthologies with important texts in normative ethics and metaethics. Here are just a few examples: Peter Singer (ed.), *A Companion to Ethics* (Oxford: Blackwell, 1993); David Copp (ed.), *The Oxford Handbook of Ethical Theory* (Oxford: Oxford University Press, 2006); and Russ Shafer-Landau (ed.), *Ethical Theory. An Anthology* (Oxford: Blackwell, 2007). An introduction to metaethics is given in Alexander Miller, *An Introduction to Contemporary Metaethics* (Cambridge: Polity Press, 2003). Russ Shafer-Landau defends moral realism in *Moral Realism: A Defence* (Oxford: Clarendon Press, 2003). A discussion for and against ethical relativism can be found in Gilbert Harman and Judith Jarvis Thomson, *Moral Relativism and Moral Objectivity* (Oxford: Blackwell, 1996). For a recent defence of emotivism (or expressivism, as he calls his view), see Alan Gibbard's *Wise Choices, Apt Feelings* (Oxford: Clarendon Press, 1990).

2

Utilitarianism

Ethics and politics

The utilitarian moral theory, urging us always to act so as to maximise the sum total of welfare among everyone affected by what we do, was stated in the eighteenth century by the English philosopher Jeremy Bentham. Bentham gathered around himself a circle of disciples, including the economist James Mill (1773–1863) and his philosophically very talented son, John Stuart Mill (1806–73). These philosophers were united not only by a common philosophical creed, but also by a social reformatory desire. They questioned traditional laws, institutions and customs, and they argued that existing systems of education, criminal justice and political institutions should be subjected to radical reform. Together with his life companion Harriet Taylor, John Stuart Mill was a pioneer in the struggle for women's liberation. His book *The Subjection of Women* (1869) soon became a classic. Bentham was also a pioneer in the fight for the interests of animals; he argued that because many animals can feel pleasure and pain just as human beings do, we have good reason to treat them no worse than we treat our fellow humans. All four were deeply involved in the task of extending the franchise to the whole of the working classes. All this is inspiring, in many ways ahead of its time and interesting in its own right, but in this chapter the exclusive focus will be on utilitarianism as such, that is, on the moral theory advocated by the utilitarians.

The utilitarian theory explained

In order to get a better grasp of utilitarianism, it would be a good idea to adopt a terminology suitable to the task. Among utilitarians it is common practice to use some moral terms in a slightly

17

technical sense. A sharp distinction is made between actions that
are right and wrong. If an action is not right, then it is wrong.
And if an action is not wrong, then it is right. The actions we
'ought' to do, or the actions that are 'obligatory' for us (these
expressions are synonymous), form a sub-class of the actions that
are right for us to do.

What does it mean when we say of an action that it is 'obligatory' or that it 'ought' to be done?

One way of explaining this would be to say that it would be
wrong not to perform this action. Note that we are speaking here
of particular actions, such as the action a certain agent performs
at a certain time (my writing this right now, for example), not
generic actions (or types of actions), such as *stealing, lying,
killing*, and so forth. Particular actions can be said to be *instances*
of generic actions. They are typically performed by individual
human beings, but they can also be performed by institutions
(such as a government) or collectives (such as a group of individuals). Note also that according to this terminology it is
possible that, in a certain situation, there are several right options
open to an agent. However, in a particular situation one alternative at most can be obligatory for an agent to perform.

Given this terminology, we can now state the utilitarian
criterion of rightness of particular actions as follows: *an action is
right if and only if in the situation there was no alternative to it
which would have resulted in a greater sum total of welfare in the
world.* Remember again that if the action is not right, then it is
wrong. This means that if there was something the agent could
have done instead of the action he or she actually performed
which would have resulted in a greater sum total of welfare in the
world, then he or she acted wrongly.

According to utilitarianism, we ought to maximise the sum
total of welfare, then. But what is it more exactly that we ought
to maximise? What does the term 'welfare' signify? On this
point utilitarians disagree. Let me briefly discuss the three most
important alternatives.

What is it that we ought to maximise?

According to classical utilitarianism we ought to maximise
happiness or well-being. This version of utilitarianism is usually
called hedonistic utilitarianism. Many contemporary utilitarians

have abandoned it, but in my opinion this is the most plausible version of utilitarianism. Furthermore, in empirical happiness studies, results of which have recently been much publicised and discussed, hedonism is more or less taken for granted. It is therefore appropriate to speak of a kind of renaissance of this idea. Let us see what it amounts to.

What is presupposed by hedonistic utilitarianism is that each sentient being, at any time, is at a certain level of well-being. We may speak of this as the hedonic situation of the individual. What matters is the hedonic situation of an individual at a given time, that is, how this situation at this moment is experienced by this person. Does it feel better than a minute ago? Does it feel roughly the same? Or does it feel worse? Questions like these are meaningful according to hedonistic utilitarianism, insofar as they identify welfare with well-being.

According to hedonistic utilitarianism, there are also situations that it is worse to experience than not to experience anything at all. What the theory presupposes is that the kind of representation of, say, the day of an individual, as shown in Figure 2.1, is meaningful. Let us assume that this is a day in my life. On the y axis we can plot the degree of well-being, and on the x axis the passage of time. The day starts when my alarm clock goes off. I leave a state of dreamless sleep and, for a moment, my situation is worse than it would have been had the alarm bell remained silent. While I brush my teeth I begin to see some meaning in my life, however, and as soon as I taste my morning coffee the situation looks quite pleasant. However, once I start to read the morning newspaper things become worse. I am reminded of the miserable state of the world (in many respects). In particular, when I read about a famine in the aftermath of the war in Somalia, I feel despair. But when I catch the tube and embark on my journey to work, once again I feel fine. However, when I leave the tube station near my office, I see a child being knocked over by a car. I rush to her rescue and for a short while I stand there, holding the unconscious child in my arms, feeling the weight of her head on my shoulder. I feel miserable. An ambulance arrives and the child is taken care of. I continue on my way to work. I start preparing a lecture. I call the hospital and learn that the child has not been injured seriously. I deliver my lecture and get a stimulating response from my audience. I go home by tube and prepare the dinner. My wife, who is a nurse at the hospital,

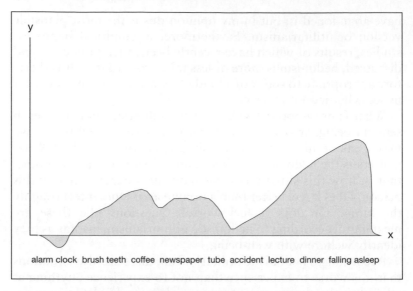

Figure 2.1 The measurement of well-being

returns home in the evening. We have dinner together, I tell her about the accident, and we go to bed early. The last thing I feel, as wakefulness merges into unconsciousness, is intense well-being.

This narrative and Figure 2.1 representing its hedonistic aspect are meaningful, according to hedonism. What is plotted on the y axis is how I experience my situation at each moment, 'from inside', so to speak. The (grey) area between the curve and the x axis can be said to represent the sum total of my well-being on this day.

It is sometimes said that hedonistic utilitarianism is incoherent since it operates with scales that are hard to reconcile. Even if, from a hedonistic point of view, pleasure is positive and pain negative, how can we assess *how* positive and *how* negative these feelings are, and how can we calculate their respective contribution to the total hedonistic state of a person at a certain moment? But the version of hedonism stated here does not presuppose that we have to perform such calculations. According to the interpretation of hedonistic utilitarianism discussed here, it is assumed that there is only *one* hedonistic dimension of our lives. At each moment we feel what we feel and that is it. Our degree of pleasure is a quality of our total experience.

It is certainly true that all sorts of experiences can contribute to the hedonistic state I am in at a certain moment. While listening to the comments from my students I remember what it felt like to hold the child in my arms and I can also look forward to tonight's supper, and so forth. All this contributes to bringing me into the hedonic state where, as a matter of fact, I am at present. This does not mean that I try to ascribe an independent value to my memory of holding the child, or listening to the comments of my students and looking forward to supper respectively, in order to *calculate* what kind of state I am in right now. I am in the state in which I am, and this is something I directly *experience*.

The fact that I directly experience what hedonic situation I am in does not presuppose that I can always make correct judgements about my hedonistic state. It is true enough that, at any time, I feel what I feel, but this does not mean that my description of my state must be correct. And when I compare the state I am in right now with the state I was in some time ago, I may very well reach the wrong conclusion. However, what is presupposed by hedonistic utilitarianism is that there is a truth in the matter (there is a fact of the matter to be right or wrong about, when I describe it).

Bentham was a straightforward hedonistic utilitarian. According to his version of utilitarianism, what should be maximised is the sum total of felt well-being (happiness). J. S. Mill did not concur with this simple form of hedonistic utilitarianism. According to him, we should distinguish between higher and lower qualities of well-being, and according to his form of utilitarianism, we should seek to maximise higher forms of well-being rather than lower ones – it is better to be a dissatisfied Socrates than a satisfied fool. And he constructed a test which should enable us to decide whether a satisfaction is of a high or a low quality: consult an individual who has experienced both, he said, and accept the verdict of this person. A person who has both read Ovid's *Ars Amatoria* and watched porn movies can tell what kind of pornography engenders the highest form (if any) of pleasure. We ought to go for the higher quality rather than the lower one.

But can the test really guide us? What if two persons reach conflicting verdicts on a certain kind of pleasure, which of them are we to trust? In particular, how do we know that they have had the *same* experience? The same stimulus can have produced different reactions in them. Moreover, even if the test works, why abide by it? Why search the higher pleasure rather than the lower, if the lower *feels* better? Suppose that a mentally retarded person feels pleasures of a lower kind than does a Nobel prize laureate, but feels them more intensely – is it really true that the Nobel prize laureate leads a better life?

A more radical departure from classical hedonism than the one taken by Mill would be to say that what matters is not that we have pleasurable experiences (a high degree of well-being), but that we get our preferences, or wishes, satisfied. This gives a different twist to Mill's test. If we *prefer* higher pleasures to lower ones, then this is a reason for us to seek higher pleasures. But according to this view, it is not only pleasures that are of importance.

We may seek all sorts of things other than certain experiences. If we do and our desires are satisfied, then we enjoy a high level of welfare. The more our desires are satisfied, the better.

We may now speak of 'preference' utilitarianism rather than 'hedonistic' utilitarianism (and of a 'preferentialist' rather than a 'hedonist' notion of welfare).

In order to be a plausible alternative to hedonism, preferentialism must be qualified. A standard qualification is as follows: only the satisfaction of preferences, or desires, that we hold for our own lives (self-regarding preferences) are of importance to our welfare; moreover, only the satisfaction of intrinsic preferences (preferences for things we want for their own sake, not merely as means to some other end) matter. The rationale behind these stipulations is as follows. Suppose I want to discover a vaccine against HIV and do so. This need not mean that my welfare has increased. But if it was essential for me that I should be the person who discovered the vaccine and did so, then it is plausible to say that my welfare has increased. However, this presupposes that I had an intrinsic desire to be the person who discovered the vaccine. This may seem to be a strange kind of desire. Perhaps it is more plausible to assume that what I was after was fame, an academic career, or something like that. But why did I seek fame and an academic career? Perhaps because I thought it would make me happy – in that case, it is only when my intrinsic desire for happiness is satisfied that my welfare is increased. But of course, people may have all sorts of self-regarding intrinsic desires. They may desire knowledge, friendship, and so on. According to preference utilitarianism, it is the satisfaction of these preferences that should be maximised.

Note that it may well be the case that some of these preferences become satisfied without the person holding them ever noticing that this is the case. Hedonists often point to this fact as a defect in the preferentialist position, but preferentialists tend to see it as a strength in their position.

A special problem with preferentialism is that we often abandon preferences. Does this mean that their satisfaction no longer matters to our welfare? Preferentialists disagree on this point. In my opinion, the most plausible move for preferentialists to make here is to say that what matters to our welfare is that our preferences get satisfied at the time when we hold them, not otherwise.

This means that satisfying somebody's wishes about what is to happen after their death will not increase their welfare. This seems to me to be the correct conclusion to draw, but note that many preferentialists have held that what makes their view plausible is indeed that, in contradistinction to hedonism, it can explain why we ought to satisfy the wishes of deceased people.

However, if they want to stick to an interpretation of their view which has this implication, they have difficulty in explaining why we should not, when we are old, satisfy preferences or desires we held as young people (concerning old age) that we gave up long ago, now that the time has come to satisfy them.

Both hedonism and preferentialism present us with subjectivist notions of welfare. Some have found these notions much too superficial. They have tried to develop a more objectivist notion of welfare, based on some kind of objective list of properties that can characterise a life worth living. Let me call such notions 'perfectionist'. Among the items on the perfectionist's list we find such things as knowledge, close relations, friendship and achievements of various kinds. According to perfectionism, my welfare is increased when I acquire important knowledge or friends, or achieve certain things.

The American Harvard philosopher Robert Nozick (1938–2002) famously put forward his experience-machine argument against hedonism in defence of a perfectionist notion of welfare. We are asked to assume that if we plug into the experience machine, then neuropsychologists can stimulate our brains so that we think and feel that we are writing great novels, or making friends or reading interesting books. Yet all the time we are floating in a tank with electrodes attached to our brains.

According to Nozick, we do not want to plug into this kind of machine. And there is a lesson to be learnt from this fact:

> We learn that something matters to us in addition to experience by imagining an experience machine and then realizing that we would not use it. (*Anarchy, State, and Utopia*, p. 44)

He then goes on to state what it is that matters to us:

> Perhaps what we desire is to live (an active verb) ourselves, in contact with reality. (Ibid., p. 45)

Is Nozick right about this? Would no one opt for the experience-machine? Perhaps some people would, after all, do so. Remember that many people resort to all kinds of drugs to enhance their mood, at least temporarily. Moreover, even if Nozick is right that we would not opt for the machine, does this show that the machine is not good for us? It seems as though in his argument for perfectionism Nozick has taken the truth of preferentialism for granted!

However, even if Nozick's argument is flawed, his conclusion may well be correct. Perhaps a life in contact with reality is better for the person living it than a life without such contact, even if it feels worse. I leave it to the reader to decide. In what follows, when various different arguments against utilitarianism are considered, nothing is dependent on an exact interpretation of the notion of welfare. So the reader is advised to opt for the version of utilitarianism which gives, in his or her opinion, the theory the best shot.

Objections to utilitarianism

Utilitarianism can seem trivially true. Who can object to the dictum that we ought to maximise welfare? Who can argue that we should sometimes act in a way that does not maximise welfare? In particular, this may be hard to understand if we are free to select our own favoured notion of welfare. However, the theory is far from self-evidently true. It can also be stated as a version of the doctrine that the end justifies the means. And this is no trivial truth. I shall now examine the most important objections to the theory and indicate how a utilitarian would attempt to answer them. It is up to the reader to decide whether the answers to the objections are convincing. Some of the objections can be said to hint in the direction of other moral theories that have been considered capable of handling the objections in a more satisfactory manner. I will return to these objections in later chapters. But one objection has been considered a knockdown objection to utilitarianism as such, without hinting at any alternative theories in particular. This objection, the first one, will be discussed at some length in the present chapter.

The objections to utilitarianism I will consider are the following:

- utilitarianism is impossible to apply;
- utilitarianism is a threat to close relations and friendship;
- utilitarianism is too demanding;
- utilitarianism is too permissive;
- utilitarianism does not take the question of equality seriously.

Can utilitarianism be applied?

According to utilitarianism we ought to maximise welfare and take into consideration any creature who is or who could be affected by our actions. Is it possible to take into account anything like this when we decide how to act? The consequences of our actions persist for an almost indefinite time and may well affect an enormous number of creatures. Moreover, it is not only the impact on sentient beings after we have acted that affects the normative status of our action (as right or wrong), but also what would have happened had we (somehow) acted differently. This may seem even more difficult to survey. Is it possible for us to apply the utilitarian criterion and to act in conformity with it?

In a way it is always possible for us to act correctly. For, as was pointed out by Immanuel Kant (to be discussed in Chapter 4), 'ought' implies 'can', and this also means that if we cannot perform a certain action, we need not do so. So all actions that are right according to utilitarianism, or any other reasonable moral theory, are performable for us. But it seems that this is of little use to us, since we cannot know which actions are right and which are wrong if utilitarianism is correct.

I think all utilitarians are prepared to concede this point. However, they do not see it as decisive. Their standard move in relation to the difficulty just brought to our attention is as follows. What matters from a utilitarian point of view is not so much that we always perform right actions but that, on the whole, we produce as good consequences as possible. And a way of doing this is to develop some kind of *decision procedure* allowing us at least to do our best in terms of the utilitarian goal.

The decision procedure that most naturally comes to mind is the following: try to account for the most important alternatives facing you, make an assessment of what the possible outcomes of each alternative are, try to assess how probable these outcomes are, on the assumption that you carry out each one, and carry out the alternative that maximises the *expected* (rather than the actual) welfare. When you make these calculations, focus on the knowledge you possess and assume that what you do not know anything about and cannot gain knowledge about (at least not in time for the decision facing you) is of no importance to your decision.

Here is an example of how this decision procedure could function: suppose you find that you face two main alternatives in a situation, to implement H1 or H2. Suppose you know that H1 will almost certainly lead to a slightly undesirable outcome, while nothing disastrous can happen if you do it. Suppose you know too that if you implement H2, then this will probably lead to much better consequences, but that you also fear that if you do H2, this may lead to disaster. Now, it is very plausible that the actual consequences of H2 are better than the actual consequences of H1, but it would not be wise to implement H2. It would simply be too risky.

But what does 'too risky' mean? Well, according to the method envisaged here it means that the sum of the products of probabilities and values for the possible outcomes of a certain action are not high enough; there exists a better alternative with a better sum of products of probabilities and values. This is represented in Figure 2.2.

To make the example more concrete. Suppose that one dark night I am in charge of a nuclear plant. I know that if I sleep towards the end of my shift I will feel fine tomorrow (worth +200 to me). On the other hand, if I stay awake, I will feel lousy tomorrow (worth −1 to me). However, if I stay awake, then I can be certain that no accident will occur. If I go to sleep, on the other hand, there is a small probability that an accident will occur and, without my intervention, will result in a disaster (this is likely to happen, I believe, with a 5 per cent probability). The value of this

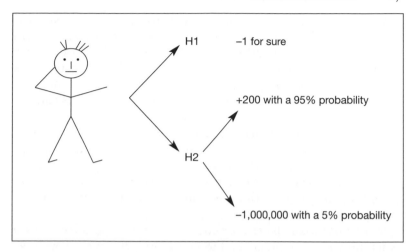

H1   −1 for sure

+200 with a 95% probability

H2

−1,000,000 with a 5% probability

Figure 2.2   To maximise expected welfare

disaster adds up to −1,000,000, when everyone affected by it has been taken into account. Now, probably, sleeping would be the right course of action for me in this situation from the point of view of utilitarianism, but to follow it would be irresponsible.

The reason is that the expected welfare of staying awake is −1 (for sure), while the expected welfare of going to sleep is (95 per cent of 200) − (5 per cent of 1,000,000) = −49,810. According to a sophisticated utilitarian, we ought to apply the decision procedure sketched above (with some provisos to be made in the next section), when making decisions on what to do.

This may seem a reasonable course of action. But why, more precisely, should we adopt it if we believe the utilitarian criterion of rightness to be correct? If we apply the decision procedure described here, we will undoubtedly often perform wrong actions rather than right actions. The answer given by the utilitarians must be along the following lines. By consistently adopting the procedure sketched here (of trying to maximise expected welfare) we produce better results on the whole than we would do if we were to act in accordance with any other method of decision-making that we could think of. It is not obvious that this answer is satisfactory.

However, a utilitarian who has to resort to a decision procedure like the one just described is faced with an even more radical objection. According to this objection, utilitarianism cannot be applied even indirectly because the values assumed above, when the method of maximisation of expected welfare was introduced, are bogus or, according to this objection, values like these are meaningless. It may be meaningful to say that it is better for me to be asleep than to be awake provided that no accident occurs, but the use of exact numbers here is misleading. These numbers (+200 and −1 respectively) are meaningless. Even more absurd is the number −1,000,000 for the value of a nuclear disaster. It is taken for granted that this number somehow represents the sum total of the loss of welfare that affects an aggregate of many persons. Such numbers are devoid of meaning, according to this objection. No interpersonal comparisons of welfare are possible.

Most utilitarians have conceded that it is impossible to give exact measures in practice. However, in principle, they have tended to claim that the differences are real. And we can also do a lot in practical life to come to reasonable approximations of them. It would be absurd to claim, for example, that those who suffered hardship in a Nazi concentration camp did not enjoy less welfare than most of you who are reading this text. We *know* that our hedonistic situation is *much* better than theirs. But approximations are only possible if there is something to approximate, that is, if there are realities that can be given a rough representation. What are the realities here? Utilitarians disagree about the answer to this question, of course, and how greatly they disagree depends on their different notions of welfare.

A classical hedonist like Bentham would argue like this. Returning to Figure 2.1, which represents a day in my life, consider a point in the diagram – say, when I brush my teeth. Where should we plot this situation on the y axis? Well, this depends, according to an idea put forward by Bentham and followed up in more detail by the economist Francis Ysidro Edgeworth (1845–1926), on how many times my hedonic situation could be worsened in a just noticeable way from where I am right now (when I brush my teeth) to the point where my life is no longer worth experiencing. This number is not accessible to us in practice, of course, but if we could construct, say, some kind of experience machine of a slightly different design from the one discussed by Nozick, then we might perhaps be able to find out. This number would measure my hedonic situation at this moment. A just noticeable difference of well-being, during the shortest possible unit of time, is the hedonistic atom, the *hedon*, that is, the unit in the hedonic calculus. And the value of this unit is the same for every person, and for the same person at different times, according to Edgeworth. The hedonistic zero is repesented at the point where it becomes better not to experience life than to experience it.

Adherents of preferentialism give other answers to the objection that comparisons of welfare in general, and interpersonal comparisons of welfare in particular, are impossible. They tend to invoke our capacity for identifying with others when making interpersonal comparisons of welfare. According to this view, we ought, figuratively speaking, to transform interpersonal comparisons into intrapersonal ones. A comparison between whether Lisa would be more satisfied with a certain gift than Peter would be with another gift involves making both Lisa's and Peter's preferences your own and then making up your mind about which preference you would like most to have satisfied. The influential Oxford philosopher R. M. Hare (1919–2002) as well as the Nobel Economics laureate John Harsanyi (1920–2000) have both developed this idea in more detail.

On the perfectionist notion of welfare the comparisons of welfare become even more complicated, of course, but perhaps it is still possible to make them in principle and also sometimes in practice, at least in an approximate manner. This is, however, obviously a highly disputed question.

Does utilitarianism threaten close relations and friendship?

The objection that utilitarianism cannot be applied was met by those who wanted to defend it with the invocation of a distinction between, on the one hand, the utilitarian criterion of rightness and, on the other, a utilitarian method of decision-making. According to the former an action is right if and only if it maximises the sum total of welfare in the universe. The latter invites us to account for the alternatives facing us, so that we can try to maximise expected rather than actual welfare. But what if we always use this method of decision-making (to the extent that it is possible for us to do so)? Does not this mean that we become rather odious creatures, callously calculating the outcome of our actions? Does not this mean that we become incapable of having close relations as well as friends? Does not this mean that the utilitarian method of decision-making has turned out to be counterproductive?

There exists a possible and very radical utilitarian answer to this objection: if the objection is sound, then forget the method of decision-making. Yes, if necessary, forget everything you have heard about the utilitarian criterion of rightness as well. This criterion may well be correct, but if it is, and if the consequences of knowing this are bad, then try to ensure that you forget that you have ever heard about it. And if this is not possible, at least do not tell your children about it! Or keep it a secret among a narrow circle of enlightened individuals.

This answer to the objection was hinted at by the Cambridge philosopher Henry Sidgwick (1838–1900) in his monumental work on ethical theory, *The Methods of Ethics*. Actually, this book is so long and complex that it is bound be read by only a few, very dedicated persons – he hence came close to keeping his theory a secret! Many people have found this answer less than satisfactory, however.

There is no need go too deeply into this question, for there are less radical and therefore more plausible defences against the objection available for the utilitarian. This is a more reasonable one: to the extent that the consequences of calculating the consequences and aiming for maximisation of expected welfare are bad, avoid it. However, when the consequences of such an attitude are positive, abide by it. Follow it when you take political decisions, for example, or when you consider seriously what to do with the rest of your life. But abstain from using it when driving your car (since there is no time for calculation when driving) and, more importantly in the present context, abstain from using the method when you are socialising with those who are near and dear to you and in your dealings with your friends. Close relations and friendship are similar in that they require a certain amount of partiality. Utilitarianism is a morality of impartiality. But it may be true that the world is a better place if people sometimes are somewhat partial. To the extent that this is true, be partial. Do not always consider whether you could exchange your spouse or your children for something better!

Does this answer the objection? There is no unanimity about this. Some tend to argue that a friendship that is, in this way, conditional is not a true friendship. And spontaneity exhibited in your relationship with your children, which you 'allow' yourself to exhibit because you believe that some degree of spontaneity has beneficial consequences, is not true spontaneity. A utilitarian father or friend must suffer from a strange kind of 'schizophrenia', often acting without regard for what he believes is a true morality. Such a father or friend is a poor father or friend.

Many adherents of utilitarianism have argued, however, that this kind of moral 'schizophrenia' is perfectly in order. It is true, they claim, that in our relations to those closest to us and friends we ought to be somewhat spontaneous and partial, but there should always be a limit to this spontaneity and partiality. We may go too far in our partiality, say. Our friend may become a devoted adherent of a repellent racist ideology, in which case the correct thing to do is not to continue to defend him, but to end the relationship. A belief in utilitarianism, with the kind of conditional spontaneity and partiality it brings with it, allows us to strike a balance between, on the one hand, loyalty, and, on the other hand, a readiness to criticise and break up. We ought from time to time to step back from our relations, no matter how close and personal they are, in order to ascertain that they are defensible from a moral point of view. Who would like to have a friend or parent who was not prepared to do so is the question posed by these defenders of utilitarianism.

Is utilitarianism too demanding?

Utilitarianism is obviously a very demanding theory. We have failed to live up to the demands of the theory if, at some time, we have not maximised the sum total of welfare in the universe. As soon as there is some individual suffering, some hardship that we could alleviate, we ought to do so – provided we cannot do even more good by performing an alternative action. In that case we ought to perform this action instead. We may have given up all our wealth to relieve suffering among people living in the poor parts of the world only to learn that we should have robbed a bank as well and sent the money to Oxfam. This may seem absurd, but note that this conclusion has been accepted as basically sound by many utilitarians. A vivid defence of a position like the one sketched here (but without explicit reference to utilitarianism) has been presented by the American philosopher Peter Unger. So perhaps this conclusion is not so absurd after all. However, many critics of utilitarianism have focused on this point and considered it a *reductio ad absurdum* of utilitarianism.

The utilitarian could, of course, deny that *utilitarianism* is the problem and instead blame the heavy demands on the *situation*. In a world without wars, injustices and environmental problems, utilitarianism, and hedonistic utilitarianism in particular, seems compatible with an easygoing life. Still, the world does contain wars, injustices and environmental problems, and given that it does, utilitarianism does indeed pose heavy demands on each and every one. So the objection must be taken seriously. But what does it amount to more exactly?

The British philosopher Bernard Williams (1929–2002) famously complained that utilitarianism 'alienates' us from our selves and our life projects (*Utilitarianism: For and Against*, p. 116); another British philosopher, John Mackie (1917–82), argued in a similar vein and repudiated utilitarianism as an 'ethics of fantasy'. A theory that is so demanding must turn out to be counterproductive. If we try to follow its requirements we will soon give up morality as such. It would be more reasonable, according to Mackie, to stick to a morality that imposes less stringent requirements on us:

> To identify morality with something that certainly will not be followed is a sure way of bringing it into contempt, practical contempt, which combines all too readily with theoretical respect. (*Ethics*, p. 132)

How should we assess arguments like these? In the next chapter I will follow them to their most extreme conclusion: ethical egoism. But neither Williams nor Mackie defends ethical egoism. They have only set out to temper the requirements posed by utilitarianism to some degree. Are they right in their arguments? Does utilitarianism alienate us from our selves and our projects? Must an ethical theory like utilitarianism turn out to be counterproductive? Does utilitarianism demand too much of us?

I have difficulties in accepting Williams' objection. It is certainly true that many people have life projects that are at variance with utilitarianism. Those who wanted to play string quartets during the last century, unperturbed by the smoke rising from the chimneys of the crematoria in the concentration camps, held projects conflicting with the demands placed on them by utilitarianism. And those of us who 'live high and let die', without doing anything to relieve suffering in poor parts of our world, pursuing our professional careers instead or focusing exclusively on the welfare of our own families, have life projects that conflict with the requirements imposed by utilitarianism. But this need not be the case. Informed by utilitarianism we could change our projects. We could make sure that we do enough for our own children (assuming that it is a good idea that each parent who can do so takes particular care of his or her own children) while devoting our lives in general to some worthy task such as combating infectious disease in poor countries (helping children who have no parents who can take care of them). Or we can devote our lives to the liberation of animals subjected to barbaric living conditions. Or we can become activists in the cause of bringing an end to global warming, and so forth. Then where is the alienation?

Mackie's objection remains to be answered, however. Most of us do not devote our lives to tasks like the ones just described. As a matter of fact, most of us do very little to alleviate suffering in the world. We choose to blind ourselves to the misery we see on television and we tolerate the fact that people, whom we could easily have saved, die. We eat meat that has been produced under cruel farming conditions and choose not to think about where it comes from. We pay little attention to the consequences of our way of life for the environment in the remote future. We leave it to our children to deal with the problems associated with global warming. Does the belief, if we hold such a belief, that in so doing we are acting wrongly make us act even more perversely wrongly? This is what Mackie seems to believe, but I think he is wrong.

It is true to say that if we feel that someone wants to place *unreasonably* stringent demands on us, we tend to rebel and stop taking these requirements seriously. If a traffic regulation required that we drive no faster than 20 miles per hour on a motorway, we would certainly rebel. But the reason that we would rebel, I submit, is not that the requirement is so strict, but that it is unreasonably strict. We can find no rationale behind it. We then come to despise the entire system of rules of which it forms a part. But if we see a point in the rule, such as a rule stipulating that we drive no faster than 20 miles an hour past a kindergarten, we do pay some respect to it. We may not abide by it if it is very strict, but nevertheless our awareness of the existence of the regulation makes us drive more slowly than we would if no regulation existed.

Could the same be said about the very strict demands placed on us by utilitarianism? This is a controversial question. I suppose that some would be prepared to argue that utilitarianism does not so much impose very strict demands on us as unreasonably strict demands. But they must be prepared to give *independent* arguments against utilitarianism. Why, then, are the demands from utilitarianism unreasonable? This is how they may argue. It must be wrong for me to have to devote all my efforts to improving the lot of those who are worst off in the world, if the reason that they are so poor is that other people do not give a damn about their situation. If everybody did his or her share, all problems could easily be solved. However, since other people are not pulling their weight, according to utilitarianism, I have to sacrifice all I own and care about. This is not fair.

Some utilitarians have flatly rejected this objection, claiming that we have precisely those obligations prescribed for us by utilitarianism. The requirements made on us by utilitarianism are very strict indeed, but they are perfectly reasonable. Others have felt some strength in the objection and turned to a version of utilitarianism known as 'rule utilitarianism'. According to rule utilitarianism, *we ought to act in accordance with a rule such that if everyone were to abide by it, the sum total of welfare would be maximised.* On such a version of utilitarianism it seems as though we need to contribute no more than our fair share, even when other people refrain from contributing theirs.

I will return briefly to this version of utilitarianism in Chapter 4. The reason for this is that it bears a structural similarity to an idea put forward by Kant in his defence of deontological ethics.

Is utilitarianism too permissive?

Utilitarianism is a version of the idea that the end justifies the means. One could think that if there is anything that could justify the choice of means, it must be the end. However, there may be limits to the applicability of this line of reasoning. If it is followed, what are usually described as atrocities may well be right, provided only that their consequences happen to be very good (in the very long run, say). According to this line of reasoning, what happened in the concentration camps during the twentieth century may have been warranted.

A utilitarian may answer this objection by pointing out how unlikely it is that the consequences of what went on in the concentration camps did maximise the sum total of welfare in the world. However, even so, a critic of utilitarianism may want to insist that this kind of objection is unsatisfactory. The reason that what went on in the concentration camps was wrong cannot be accidental, in the way the utilitarian has it. The wrongness of what went on must be inherent in the criminal acts themselves. They can point out that, confronted with the trolley example described in the opening chapter, the utilitarian must claim that it is right to push the big man onto the track in the Footbridge case since here we have *assumed* that there are no bad side-effects. By sacrificing (killing) him we save five lives, and this is something we ought to do, according to utilitarianism. But this conclusion is absurd, they may claim.

To a limited extent the utilitarian can endorse this kind of reasoning. A utilitarian may argue that murder in general should be strongly proscribed, and even more importantly, whenever possible, crimes against humanity should be prosecuted and punished. The rationale behind such prohibitions, of course, is that such actions are in general wrong. And even if, in some rare and highly exceptional instances, they happen to maximise the sum total of welfare (which may have been true, for example, of some acts of murder where the victims happened to be extremely nasty people), there may be good reasons to punish them. For unless we do punish all acts of murder and create strong inhibitions against them, we will always, all of us, feel insecure. We do not want to live in a world where our neighbour is prepared to consider killing us as a means of making the world a better place. So even if it is right to push the big man in the Footbridge case according to utilitarianism, the utilitarian would urge us to develop character traits that render it difficult for us to do the right thing in an exceptional situation such as this one.

Does this argument apply to abortion as well as to murder? This is not as clear. If utilitarianism is correct, some abortions may be right and some may wrong, just like acts of murder, depending on how they affect the sum total of welfare. However, even though a utilitarian wants to prohibit murder, he or she may well endorse a law granting pregnant women the right to abortion. Such a law does not pose a (felt) threat to any living person. The foetuses need not fear that they will be aborted. They cannot fear this or anything else. And we who can feel fear (and would feel a constant fear if murder was permitted) cannot be killed through abortion. So the crucial aspect of abortion law, from a utilitarian point of view, is that women can feel secure: if they want to carry their pregnancy to term, they should be allowed to do so; if they want to terminate it through abortion, they should be free to do so.

However, it should be noted that, according to utilitarianism, many abortions are in fact wrong. They are wrong for the simple reason that the aborted foetus, if it had been carried to term, could have developed into a happy person!

Is the utilitarian view of killing acceptable? Some may find that it gives the right kind of answer with respect to abortion. But even for those who accept its verdict on abortion, it may be difficult to accept the view that the wrongness of killing is mainly to do with bad consequences. And it may be difficult to accept the kind of double standards advocated by utilitarians. According to utilitarianism, some horrendous action, such as the deliberate killing of an innocent human being, may be correct (since, as a matter of fact, in the circumstances, it saves more lives than it sacrifices). And yet, for all that, these morally right acts of murder should be prohibited by criminal law and, if detected, be prosecuted and punished by criminal justice. Could this really be a sound moral stance?

Utilitarianism and equality

According to utilitarianism we ought to *maximise* the sum total of welfare. This seems to be an account that pays no respect whatever to the distribution of welfare. What if the sum total gets maximised where some person who has a very low level of welfare gets nothing at all, while those who are already well off get their situation improved? Would this be acceptable?

In principle the utilitarian has to concede that it is acceptable. It is certainly true, the utilitarian may argue, that in general we cannot maximise the sum total of welfare by favouring those who are best off. On the contrary, what economists refer to as the law of diminishing marginal utility informs us that those who are worst off are also those who have most to gain when they receive goods such as prestige, money and other material resources. So utilitarianism pays a kind of special indirect respect to those who are worst off.

However, the law of diminishing marginal utility is not always applicable. It seems to work when we discuss material goods, but not always when we speak of such things as medical resources.

We may gain more welfare by giving scarce medical resources to a person who enjoys a rather high level of welfare, suffering from a disease that could easily be cured, than by giving the same scarce resources to a person with a very low level of welfare suffering from a disease that cannot be cured and such that the effects of it can be only slightly palliated. Then, according to utilitarianism, the resource should go to the person who is already enjoying more welfare. Is this really fair?

Many people have thought that it is not. Some have argued that when resources are being distributed we should try to level out differences. Others have argued (more plausibly in my opinion) that when resources are being distributed, those who are, absolutely speaking, worst off should have a special claim.

This view is known as the 'priority' view and it comes in many versions. The most radical says that if we can improve the lot of the individual who is worst off, we should do so, irrespective of the price other people have to pay (as long as they are better off than the person who was worst off initially).

It may be thought that this is the view famously defended by the Harvard philosopher John Rawls. Does not his 'difference' principle invite us to focus exclusively on those who are worst off? However, appearances are deceptive. What Rawls is discussing is the distribution of material resources (basic goods), not welfare. And when faced with medical examples like the one given above, Rawls abstains from giving a definite verdict. And I think few would accept the priority view in its strongest version. Under certain circumstances this would lead to a situation where, in order to improve the lot of one very miserable person only slightly, all of us would have to forgo all the joys in life. This cannot be right.

However, there are less radical versions of the priority view that have attracted much sympathy in the discussion. These versions imply that we ought to pay more interest to those who are (absolutely speaking) worst off and decreasingly less interest to those who are better off.

Conclusion

This concludes the discussion of utilitarianism. Note that not all objections to it can be true. If the first objection is correct and utilitarianism is inapplicable, then the other objections must be flawed, since they complain that utilitarianism, when applied, leads to the wrong moral conclusions. Note that these other objections, when carried to their respective logical conclusions, seem to lead to other moral theories. If the complaint that utilitarianism threatens close relations and friendship is taken seriously, then we may need to have recourse to a morality focusing on traits of character rather than on criteria of right action (some kind of virtue ethics). If we find that utilitarianism puts too heavy demands on us, then we may have to resort to ethical egoism. If we want to object to the fact that utilitarianism gives us too much moral licence, allowing us to kill in order to save lives, then we may want to resort to deontology or an ethics of rights.

I now turn to these and various other alternatives to utilitarianism.

Further reading about utilitarianism

A classical statement of utilitarianism is found in Jeremy Bentham's *Principles of Morals and Legislation* (1789), which can be found in many editions. John Stuart Mill gives the first simple and systematic account of the theory in *Utilitarianism* (1861), also available in many editions. I defend hedonistic utilitarianism in my book *Hedonistic Utilitarianism* (Edinburgh: Edinburgh University Press, 1998) and Fred Feldman defends another version of the theory in *Pleasure and the Good Life* (Oxford: Oxford University Press, 2004). Robert Nozick's example with the experience-machine is described in *Anarchy, State, and Utopia* (Oxford: Blackwell, 1974). A stimulating discussion about utilitarianism is J. J. C. Smart and Bernard Williams, *Utilitarianism: For and Against* (Cambridge: Cambridge University Press, 1973), where Smart is defending utilitarianism and Williams attacking it. Books on different notions of welfare include James Griffin, *Well-Being* (Oxford: Clarendon Press, 1986); L. W. Sumner, *Welfare, Happiness, and Ethics* (Oxford: Clarendon Press, 1996); and John Broome, *Weighing*

Goods: Equality, Uncertainty, and Time (Oxford: Blackwell, 1991). Michael Stocker discusses 'moral schizophrenia' in 'The Schizophrenia of Modern Ethical Theories', reprinted in Roger Crisp and Michael Slote, *Virtue Ethics* (Oxford: Oxford University Press, 1997). The book that has meant most to recent discussions about utilitarianism, posing a lot of new riddles, is Derek Parfit's *Reasons and Persons* (Oxford: Clarendon Press, 1984). The quotation from John Mackie, where he argues that utilitarianism places too heavy demands on us, is taken from *Ethics: Inventing Right and Wrong* (Harmondsworth: Penguin, 1977). Peter Unger's defence of a morality imposing very strict demands on us is put forward in *Living High and Letting Die: Our Illusion of Innocence* (Oxford and New York: Oxford University Press, 1996). In the book many new twists are added to the trolley problem. On utilitarianism and equality, see Larry S. Temkin, *Inequality* (Oxford: Oxford University Press, 1993). John Rawls famously defends his 'difference principle', as an integral part of his complete view of social justice, in *A Theory of Justice* (Oxford: Oxford University Press, 1971). Rule-utilitarianism is presented in Brad Hooker, Elinor Mason and Dale E. Miller (eds), *Morality, Rules and Consequences: A Critical Reader* (Edinburgh: Edinburgh University Press, 2000). A famous attempt to apply hedonistic utilitarian thinking in economic theory is made by Richard Layard in *Happiness: Lessons from a New Science* (London: Allen Lane, 2005).

3

Egoism and Contractualism

Introduction

Utilitarianism makes unreasonably strict demands on us, according to one line of argument. If we follow this argument to its most
extreme conclusion, we end up with ethical egoism. According to
ethical egoism we have no duties to anyone but ourselves. This
does not mean that the entire world ought to satisfy *my* interests.
Ethical egoism is a moral theory, which can be cast in perfectly
universal terms: *according to ethical egoism, every individual
ought to satisfy his or her own best interests*. Or, to put it in terms
we know from the preceding chapter: *every individual ought to
maximise his or her own welfare*.

According to egoism, each individual has a goal of his or her
own (in utilitarianism we all share the same goal). This diversity
of goals may engender conflict. This is not an objection to ethical
egoism, however. When people have goals that conflict, each
individual ought, according to egoism, to maintain his or her own
goal. Ethical egoism is a consistent ethical theory, in competition
with other ethical theories.

We saw in the preceding chapter that utilitarians disagree
over the correct interpretation of the notion of welfare. Egoists
similarly disagree. Egoism comes in the three main versions we
already know about: hedonistic egoism, preferentialist egoism
and perfectionist egoism. What has already been said about these
three ideas of what makes a life worth living (well-being, satisfaction of preferences or objective values such as close relations,
friendship, knowledge, achievements) applies to egoism as well.

Three of the objections raised against utilitarianism can also
be directed against egoism. Can egoism really be applied? Does
it not pose rather strict duties upon us? Does it not give us too
much moral licence?

Note, however, that it is comparatively easier for the egoist to meet the objection that the moral theory in question cannot be applied. For in the first place the egoist need not bother with far-reaching consequences of his or her actions (taking place long after he or she is gone), and second, he or she need not enter into the complicated question of how to make interpersonal comparisons of welfare. In the final analysis, it is only the welfare of the agent that counts.

The objection that too heavy demands are imposed also loses much of its force when directed against egoism rather than utilitarianism. But even egoism makes strict demands on the agent. According to egoism, you act wrongly whenever you do not maximise your own best interests. This means that you make a moral mistake if you sacrifice future pleasures for inferior present ones. And you act wrongly when, in choosing a way of life, you destroy your health or shorten your life – unless you succeed in compensating for ill health and brevity of life with increased quality. It is not far-fetched to assume that often, when we say that lack of quantity is compensated in terms of quality, we are deceiving ourselves. If this is so, according to egoism, we are acting immorally. However strict these demands may be, it is perhaps plausible to claim that they are not *unreasonably* strict. At least this is a claim the adherent of ethical egoism must make.

The objection that the moral theory in question allows the agent too much moral licence has at least the same force when directed at egoism as it had when it was directed against utilitarianism. The egoist is prepared to kill, not only in order to save many lives, but in order to save his or her own life, and so forth. However, the egoist is likely to bite this bullet and is prepared to live with this implication of the theory.

It may be thought that an ethical egoist must be a very unpleasant person, but this is not true. The ethical egoist may find pleasure in helping other people; he or she may have all sorts of altruistic interests. However, once a conflict emerges it is clear how the ethical egoist, who wants to abide by his or her favoured moral theory, ought to act: he or she ought to ensure that his or her own welfare is maximised.

How would an ethical egoist respond to Foot's and Thomson's trolley cases? He or she would argue that *any* decision is right, so long as it satisfies the interests of the *agent*. And, according to the same kind of argument, if it is somehow bad for *me* to flick the switch in the first simple trolley example, I ought not to do so. It would be wrong if I saved the five persons! This may sound so strange that some may want to deny that ethical egoism is an ethical theory at all. However, as we shall see, the theory is more sophisticated than it might at first appear. Moreover, it is in competition with the other theories in this book, and since *these* theories are clearly ethical ones, I see no problem in recognising ethical egoism as an ethical theory in its own right.

Arguments in defence of egoism

One widely read author of popular novels during the second half of the last century, Ayn Rand, contributed to public interest in ethical egoism by her committed defence of the theory. Ethical egoism has also provided a philosophical rationale behind a certain kind of libertarian political ideology that was very popular at the beginning of this century. It would not be correct to say, however, that Rand puts forward any strong arguments in defence of ethical egoism. Can any be found?

Many seem to have argued along the following lines. Morality must have something to do with rationality. But does not rational action consist in prudent action; that is, does not rational action consist in actions satisfying the long-term interests of the agent himself or herself? Even the great utilitarian author Henry Sidgwick, referred to in the previous chapter, seems to have argued along these lines. This is how he puts the point:

> [E]ven if a man admits the self-evidence of the principle of Rational Benevolence, he may still hold that his own happiness is an end which it is irrational for him to sacrifice to any other. (*Methods of Ethics*, p. 498)

But this argument is mistaken. It may certainly be said that unless we maximise the satisfaction of the interests we happen to hold, our actions are irrational. This claim could be made true even through an act of fiat: we could claim that maximising one's interests is what is *meant* by acting 'rationally'. And according to this stipulation it is certainly true that, for a person who is exclusively concerned with his or her own happiness, it would be irrational not to maximise it. However, on this notion of rationality, nothing is said about the content of our interests. In a similar vein, for a person who holds an impartial interest in the welfare of all sentient beings, it would be irrational not to maximise the sum total of welfare. But what concerns ought we to have? Both utilitarianism and egoism address this question, and the theories give conflicting answers. No reference to the notion of rationality can solve this conflict, nor does it strengthen any of the respective positions.

Are there any other arguments in defence of egoism, arguments that would fare better than the rationality argument? I know of none. But this is really not bad news for ethical egoism. There were no convincing arguments in defence of utilitarianism either. In fact, there seem to be no good arguments in defence of any moral theory. We do not establish the plausibility of any moral theory by providing one decisive argument in its defence. The defence of a moral theory must be piecemeal. We find situations where the theory is in harmony with our considered moral intuitions, and we feel that it gives a good explanation of them, so we hold on to it, tentatively, until conflicting evidence comes up. When such evidence emerges we have to make a choice. How repugnant is the conclusion we have derived from the theory? What are the theoretical alternatives? What kind of theory can reasonably be chosen in the light of what we have found out? To select a moral theory is rather like selecting a scientific hypothesis; we want consistency with our considered moral intuitions, of course, but we want simplicity, generality, consistency with what we already believe we know as well.

Are there any situations where egoism matches our considered moral intuitions better than utilitarianism? This is a controversial question, but we have already seen that many believe that when utilitarianism makes in their opinion too strict demands on us, egoism is more in harmony with our considered moral intuitions. According to egoism we may continue the kind of lifestyle we have found congenial, even if this means that people in poor countries starve to death. Ethical egoism does not alienate us from our selves or from our life projects. However, there are also problems with ethical egoism, and I will now focus exclusively on them, and on attempted revisions of the theory in their light.

Arguments against egoism

It may be true that if people adopt egoism, then some major evils of the kind we know only too well from the past century will not come about. From an egoistic point of view there seems to be little reason to sacrifice one or two generations in the hope that some time in the future there will be compensation for these sacrifices. However, given egoism, it might be difficult to find reasons to make sacrifices now in order to avoid future disasters such as global warming. Moreover, egoism seems to make room for some rather nasty petty evils instead. Think of the following case. I am sitting in a tavern on the southern shore of the Mediterranean with the starry heavens above me. I am enjoying dinner in the company of my best friends. We are discussing how I should invest a fortune I have recently inherited. Then a beggar approaches us. She is obviously starving. She does not want to join our supper, but she asks me for a small contribution. She has not had anything to eat for several days, she says, and I believe her, knowing that no social security exists in the country in which I am spending my holiday. For a moment I ponder whether I should invite her to eat with us. However, I realise that if I do, I will feel uncomfortable. I will not enjoy the meal. Nevertheless, seized by a strange, momentary weakness of will, I invite her to join us. She accepts. She bolts the food down, expresses her thanks and then leaves. Did I act morally correctly? Well, according to ethical egoism it certainly seems that I did not. My action caused me unnecessary embarrassment for a brief moment. I could easily have avoided this if I had rejected the beggar's plea in the first place. It may be hard to believe that a moral theory that has this kind of implication can be correct.

It may be thought, though, that if everybody tends to his or her own concerns the result will on the whole be better for everyone. So even if we may conjure up examples like the one I presented above, they are the exception; in general, the results for all will be quite good if everybody sticks to ethical egoism. But this is not so, and this is the most serious argument against ethical egoism in its most straightforward form.

We saw in the previous chapter that many have thought that utilitarianism is self-defeating. The result will be devastating, it has been held, if everybody tries to live in accordance with utilitarianism. It is debatable whether this argument holds. But even if it does, it does not prove, as we have seen, that utilitarianism is a false doctrine. A true moral theory need not be applicable. However, it would perhaps be an argument against even the truth of a moral theory if it could be shown that if everybody succeeded in following it, its own goal must be frustrated. This cannot be shown about utilitarianism, but it can be shown about ethical egoism. There are situations such that, even if everybody succeeds in maximising his or her welfare, everybody fares worse than they would have done if they had not abided by their favoured moral theory.

The argument to this effect (which dates back to the 1950s) is known as 'the prisoner's dilemma', and I will state it very briefly. It stems from rational game theory and it is usually attributed to A. W. Tucker. This is how it is presented in a classic textbook: two suspects are taken into custody and separated. The district attorney is certain that they are guilty of a specific crime, but he does not have enough evidence to convict them in a trial. He points out to the prisoners that two alternatives are open to each of them: to confess to the crime that the police are convinced they have committed, or not to. If neither of them confesses, then he will arrest them on a very minor trumped-up charge and they will both receive a short prison sentence (one year); if they both confess they will be prosecuted, but he will recommend less than the maximum sentence (eight years); but if one confesses and the other does not, then the confessor will receive lenient treatment for turning state's evidence (three months only) whereas the other will 'get the book thrown at him' (ten years). If both prisoners are rational egoists, they will both confess and end up with eight years in gaol. For no matter what the other does, it is better for each to confess than not to confess (it is assumed that each prisoner cannot affect what the other does). If one confessed the other would do better to confess too, or else he will end up in gaol for ten years (instead of eight). And if the other has not confessed, it is even better to confess, for then one will get away with three months rather than eight years in gaol. This argument holds true for each of them. But this is really stupid. If they had both given up ethical egoism and not confessed, then each of them would have got away with one year in gaol.

Their situation can be represented as set out in Figure 3.1.

It is obvious that rational egoists end up with a bad result in situations such as the one just described. It is a special case, however. It might be thought that it could not be of much practical importance. However, even if it is of little practical importance, it does have theoretical significance. Does it not count against ethical egoism that it has this kind of implication?

Prisoner's dilemma		Prisoner 2	
		Not confess	Confess
Prisoner 1	Not confess	1 year, 1 year	10 years, 3 months
	Confess	3 months, 10 years	8 years, 8 years

Figure 3.1   The prisoner's dilemma

Moreover, even from a practical point of view this problem is important, for even if we rarely find ourselves in the kind of situation described here, we often are in situations that could be characterised as generalisations of it. When many people interact in a rather anonymous modern society, they often face situations that are in important respects like the prisoner's dilemma. We face such situations when we contemplate how we should dispose of our litter at a picnic, we face them when we consider whether we should drive our own car or travel by public transport, and so forth. In such situations each person has something to gain by leaving litter behind or driving his or her own car, irrespective of what others do.

But if many people leave their litter (causing environmental damage) or drive their own cars (causing traffic jams and adding to global warming), the situation of each will be worse than it would have been if they had all disposed of their litter carefully or opted for public transport. Situations such as these are often referred to as social dilemmas, and they are the rule rather than the exception. Given the existence of many social dilemmas, rational egoism begins to seem like a version of collective stupidity.

However, the problem just noted may perhaps engender a solution for egoism: why not contract with each other in order to get out of the problem just described?

Contractualism

Thomas Hobbes must have had some intuitive grasp of the prisoner's dilemma. Hobbes did indeed think that human beings should act egoistically, but this is not of much importance in the present context. It is more important to note that he thought that, as a matter of fact, man is egoistic. And this lays the ground for problems, according to Hobbes. His belief in psychological egoism, the doctrine that, as a matter of fact, man is driven by a zeal for his own welfare, may have been somewhat exaggerated. Bishop Joseph Butler (1692–1752) famously rejected psychological egoism in his *Fifteen Sermons*. It is obvious that Butler was right. Human beings do not always maximise their own welfare. First of all, they often fail to face up to the rather strict requirements imposed by ethical egoism: they drink alcohol, neglect their own health, and so forth. Second, they are often motivated to take care of the welfare of others, even if this means that they have to make sacrifices. In particular, human beings seem to be capable of making sacrifices in the interest of their own children. And yet, for all that, it may still be true that there are severe limits to our capacity for altruistic care.

Perhaps the following picture, drawn by the Scottish Enlightenment philosopher David Hume (1711–76), is more realistic:

> [F]ar from thinking, that men have no affection for any thing beyond themselves, I am of opinion, that tho' it be rare to meet with one, who loves any single person better than himself; yet 'tis as rare to meet with one, in whom all the kind affections, taken together, do not overbalance all the selfish. (*A Treatise of Human Nature*, p. 538)

But even such restricted affection for others may engender problems like the prisoner's dilemma. Remember that the kind of problem posed by the prisoner's dilemma arises as soon as people have *different* goals for their actions. Hume was well aware of this:

> For while each person loves himself better than any other single person, and in his love to others bears the greatest affection to his relations and acquaintances, this must necessarily produce an opposition of passions, and a consequent opposition of actions; which cannot but be dangerous to the new-establish'd union. (Ibid., p. 539)

An objection could be raised to this account of our human predicament that even if we often act egoistically, or show preferential concern for those who are near and dear, this does not show that we must do so. Furthermore, even if we often act egoistically, this does not show that we *ought* to do so. However, I think it fair to take both Hobbes and Hume as saying that we cannot help acting somewhat egoistically. And while it is certainly true that this does not show that we ought to do so, it does still show that we are allowed to do it. For, as was noted in the previous chapter, according to Kant's famous and very plausible dictum, 'ought' implies 'can'. But if 'ought' implies 'can', this also means that if we cannot do a certain act, we need not do it.

Does all this mean that conventional morality is beyond rescue, or at least that the only plausible morality is ethical egoism? And if so, is this not extremely bad news if egoism leads to suboptimal solutions in social dilemmas? Does this not mean that we are forever doomed to live in what Hobbes called a state of nature? A state characterised by:

> no place for industry, because the fruit thereof is uncertain: and consequently no culture of the earth; no navigation, nor use of the commodities that may be imported by sea; no commodious building; no instruments of moving, and removing, such things as require much force; no knowledge of the face of the earth; no account of time; no arts; no letters; no society; and which is worst of all, continual fear, and danger of violent death; and the life of man, solitary, poor, nasty, brutish, and short. (*Leviathan*, ch. 13)

However, once we realise how nasty a state of nature must be, we can find a way out, according to Hobbes. Rational egoists must come to invent some kind of political authority (Hobbes called the state 'Leviathan', which is the name of a biblical monster) with a capacity to *enforce* cooperation in situations like the prisoner's dilemma. This may seem to be a move out of the frying pan into the fire. We exchange the state of nature for a totalitarian regime. Is there no way that rational egoists can freely cooperate in situations like the prisoner's dilemma?

To some extent they can. During the 1980s the following solution was much discussed, and made influential, in political philosophy through a book by Robert Axelrod called *The Evolution of Cooperation*. In what has been called repeated prisoner's dilemma situations, rational egoists can adopt what Axelrod called a 'tit-for-tat' strategy. A repeated prisoner's dilemma situation is a situation just like the original prisoner's dilemma situation, but such that there is a chance that the adversaries will meet again, under similar conditions. The tit-for-tat strategy can be described as follows. When you meet a stranger in a situation like the prisoner's dilemma, try to cooperate with him or her, then respond in kind to the opponent's previous action. If there is a certainty that you will meet again, then this strategy is successful. However, there are severe limits to the applicability of the tit-for-tat strategy.

First of all, there must not exist any exact number of encounters that the adversaries know will take place in the future. For in that case each also knows that, in the last encounter, the other person will not cooperate. But through a line of backward inductive reasoning this argument also has an impact on the meeting before the next, and the meeting before this meeting, and so forth, to a meeting where each person knows that the other will not cooperate ... up to the encounter taking place right now.

Second, and even more importantly, the tit-for-tat strategy is successful only if people cooperate with each other in paired encounters. If many people are each trying to find a strategy that works in cooperation with all the rest, then the tit-for-tat strategy fails. What has been known as 'free-riding', that is, acting in accordance with short-term egoistic interests, taking advantage if possible of those who cooperate, becomes a reasonable strategy for each person to adopt. And note that most real-life situations like the prisoner's dilemma are of the many-persons variety.

But could not morality do the trick? Could we not contract to have a certain morality that spurs us to cooperate freely? As a matter of fact, this is how Hobbes tried to solve the problem. According to him, to some extent people must be forced by the government to cooperate; the state must supervise their actions and if they fail to abide by the rules of law, threaten them with all sorts of punishment. But this does not help people to keep their promises when they know that they can break the rules and get away with it. Hobbes noted this and yet, for all that, he seems to have believed that rational egoists must realise that they all stand to gain from a morality that makes them cooperate even when they can defect and avoid the consequences. So to the extent that they are rational, even egoists will come to abide by such a morality.

This is a very attractive view of morality. It does not presuppose that people are any better than they really are. In a manner of speaking, contractualism accepts that we are incorrigible egoists and gives up conventional morality – but only to invent it once again, as the solution to a cooperation problem for rational egoists.

But does contractualism work? Why should rational egoists keep their word if they know that they can break it without fear of retribution?

Here is Hobbes' answer to this question, posed by another fictitious character he invented, the Foole. The Foole claims that it is reasonable to deceive those who help him when he knows that this will go unnoticed, but Hobbes protests:

> [H]e which declares he thinks it reason to deceive those that help him, can in reason expect no other means of safety, than what can be had from his own single Power. He therefore that breaketh his Covenant ... cannot be received into any Society, that unite themselves for Peace and Defence, but by the errour of them that receive him; nor when he is received, be retayned in it, without seeing the danger of their errour; which errours a man cannot reasonably reckon upon as means of his security. (*Leviathan*, ch. 15)

Hobbes' own answer to the Foole is less than convincing. If the Foole is successful, why should he not break the covenant? However, in modern versions of contractualism attempts have been made to strengthen Hobbes' answer. The most important attempt goes along the following lines.

It is certainly true that if I am a rational egoist and I have an opportunity to deceive others and get away with it, then this is, according to ethical egoism, what I ought to do. However, it is not a good idea to be a person who deceives others in situations like this. Such an individual will be ostracised. No one will want to have anything to do with such a person.

But if such people deceive others and get away with it, does this not mean that they will be accepted into all sorts of communities after all, even when they have deceived others? If they are clever enough only to deceive others where this goes unnoticed, how could this be detrimental to their interests?

Well, it is likely that it is still detrimental to their interests, even if, in each instance, they get away with their deception. For people are not only recognised by their deeds. People have characters as well. And we are reasonably good at exposing one another. Even if you can deceive me on one particular occasion and get away with it, you will need to have a certain kind of character. And it is likely that I will recognise you for the person you are, irrespective of whether, in this particular case, I can detect your deception. If not transparent, people are at least semi-transparent. And this fact gives each of us a reason to develop reliable traits of character.

Note that if this argument is sound, then it may be a good idea for rational egoists to try to become the kind of people who keep their word even when they can break it, gain by this and get away with it. This certainly means that in a specific situation where they keep their word they do not maximise their own welfare. However, when deciding to become people who do not always maximise their welfare, their decision certainly is in accordance with the demands of ethical egoism.

This kind of argument in defence of Hobbes' answer to the Foole has been developed most famously by the Canadian philosopher David Gauthier (in a book with the telling title *Morals by Agreement*). The argument is subtle and, to some extent at least, it is probably sound. However, to what exact extent it is sound is debatable. How far is it possible for us to decide, in general, about our own traits of character? In particular, if deep down we are egoists, can we really develop *stable* characters of the required kind? This is a theme to which I will return in Chapter 6, which deals explicitly with virtue ethics. Moreover, to what extent is it possible for us to see through each other's character? When Gauthier accepts the fact that, basically, we are rational egoists, he can be described as giving a rather pessimistic picture of humanity. When at the same he claims that we are good at detecting each other's true character, he can be said to be giving a rather optimistic picture. Both the pessimistic and the optimistic parts of his moral psychology can be, and have been, questioned.

Moral objections to contractualism based on egoism

Even if it could be shown that a contractualism based on ethical egoism is capable of handling the kind of practical problems discussed above, some moral objections remain to be answered. Note the complete amorality in its point of departure. We ought each of us to maximise our own welfare or, at least, this is something we are allowed to do (since we cannot help doing it anyway). This idea that we cannot help furthering our own interests was Hobbes' point of departure, to which some modern advocates of a contractual morality have concurred, such as, for example, the American Nobel laureate and economist James Buchanan. According to this egoistic version of contractualism, nothing but rational self-interest can make the contracting parties accede to the demands made by other contracting parties. And, once again, nothing but rational self-interest can make them develop traits of character such that, in some situations, they somewhat modify their greed. Is all this acceptable from a moral point of view?

Is it really true, as some contractual philosophers have argued, that once conventional morality is given up and exchanged for a contractual morality based on ethical egoism, much of its content will come back to us, only in a new form? Must not, on the contrary, a social contract between rational egoists be extremely unequal? Must not the terms of the contract come to favour those who are strong and disfavour those who are weak?

Hobbes himself confronted this question and thought that it could be met along the following lines. Even if some people are cleverer or stronger than others, it is still the case that no one is so much cleverer or stronger than the others that he or she cannot be brought down by them if they act in concert. This means that even if the terms of the contract are somewhat unequal, they will be equal enough. But this answer is not convincing.

First of all, some human beings are so weak that they have nothing to contribute when the contract is set up. I think here of severely disabled people and of people living in abject poverty in poor parts of the world. They have to rely, if we follow the contractual line of argument with its basis in rational egoism, on charity if they want their situation to be improved. If they are treated badly, ethical egoism (even in its contractual form) gives them no ground for a moral complaint.

Second, there are many non-human creatures that are incapable of taking part in the contract. All these creatures, that is, all sorts of sentient beings capable of feeling pain but completely devoid of cunning, will have to rely for their welfare on the goodwill of those who draw up the moral contract. If, as a matter of fact, they are treated badly, there is no ground for moral criticism if ethical egoism is sound. Does not this count against the plausibility of egoism (even in its contractual form)?

Finally, future generations seem to be at the mercy of the

present generation if ethical egoism (even in the contractual form) is basically sound. There is no way that the present generation can cooperate with future generations. The present generation can in so many ways harm the interests of future generations, but future generations can in no way retaliate. This means that all future generations are always at the mercy of the present generation if ethical egoism (even in its contractual form) is sound.

Is there any way for the adherent of ethical egoism to answer these moral objections? There seem to be two main ways for the ethical egoist to deal with them.

On the one hand, the ethical egoist can bite the bullet and argue that this is as far as our moral obligation can take us. If disabled people, poor people in poor countries, sentient non-human animals and future generations get sacrificed in the interest of the present generation of ordinary human beings who are living high at present in the rich part of the world, then so be it. There is no ground for any moral complaint.

On the other hand, the ethical egoist can try to play down the importance of the objections. One way of doing this would be to give reasons to the effect that ordinary human beings will, as a matter of course, care for disabled people (in particular if they are related to them). They will help poor people in poor parts of the world (in particular if their misery becomes visible to them through the media). They will refrain from being cruel to non-human creatures (in particular if they can sympathise with them). And, as a matter of course, they will take the interest of future generations into account. After all, these future generations will be the offspring of the offspring ... of the present generation.

Conclusion

We have seen that ethical egoism, even in its contractual version, faces many problems. Some are theoretical (how can ethical egoism deal with situations like the prisoner's dilemma?), others are downright moral (does it give weak human beings, sentient non-human beings, or future generations their due?).

One way of answering the moral objections is, as we have seen, to play down their importance. Is this move satisfactory? Some may want to argue that, for example, disabled or poor people have a *right* to decent treatment. But this treatment should not be the result of an act of charity. I will return to this line of argument in Chapter 5, where I discuss theories of *moral rights*.

Others would repeat the moral argument raised against utilitarianism: ethical egoism gives too much moral licence to the agent. We ought not to focus on the consequences of our actions, they would argue, but rather on the act itself. There are obligations and prohibitions facing a moral agent that have nothing whatsoever to do with the consequences of his or her action.

In the next chapter I move on to a discussion of this kind of *deontological* morality.

Further reading about egoism

The best monograph on ethical egoism is Jan Österberg's *Self and Others* (Dordrecht: Kluwer Academic Publishers, 1988). Defences of ethical egoism are given in T. R. Machan, *Human Rights and Human Liberties: A Radical Reconsideration of the American Political Tradition* (Chicago: Nelson Hall, 1975) and Eric Mack, 'Egoism and Rights Revisited', *The Personalist*, vol. 58, 1977. Ayn Rand defends a version of egoism in *The Virtue of Selfishness: A New Concept of Egoism* (New York: New American Library, 1964). An instructive reflection on egoism and the possibility of altruism is given in Thomas Nagel, *The Possibility of Altruism* (Princeton, NJ: Princeton University Press, 1970). The quotation from Henry Sidgwick is from *The Methods of Ethics* (New York: Dover Publications, 1966). My example of the prisoner's dilemma is from R. D. Luce and H. Raiffa, *Games and Decisions* (New York: Wiley & Sons, 1957). A simple introduction to decision theory is Michael D. Resnik, *Choices: An Introduction to Decision Theory* (Minneapolis: University of Minnesota Press, 1987). Thomas Hobbes' classic statement of contractualism is given in *Leviathan* (1651), available in many editions. David Hume, *A Treatise of Human Nature* (1739–40) is also available in many editions. The quotations here are taken from the Penguin edition (1969). Bishop Joseph Butler's argument against psychological egoism is presented in *Fifteen Sermons* (1726). Robert Axelrod argues for the tit-for-tat strategy in *The Evolution of Cooperation* (New York: Basic Books, 1984). P. Molander shows in 'The Prevalence of Free Riding', in *Journal of Conflict Resolution*, vol. 36, 1992, that the tit-for-tat strategy has restricted application. Modern statements of contractualism based on ethical egoism are found in David Gauthier, *Morals by Agreement* (Oxford: Clarendon Press, 1986) and in J. M. Buchanan, *The Limits of Liberty: Between Anarchy and Leviathan* (Chicago: Chicago University Press, 1975). It should be noted, finally, that when I speak of 'contractualism' in this chapter, I have in mind a literal sense of the word: people negotiate to find solutions to common problems. 'Contractualism' is also the name of a way of *justifying* moral theories, with reference to what people *would* agree about, under certain idealised conditions. John Rawls, mentioned in the previous chapter, can then be described as a 'contractualist' as well. This is a *metaethical* notion of contractualism, however, and it is not further discussed in this book.

4

Deontological Ethics

Introduction

The moral theories I have discussed in the previous chapters, utilitarianism and ethical egoism, are sometimes called 'consequentialist', since they claim that the value of the consequences of our actions (for everyone affected or for ourselves) is decisive for their moral status (as right or wrong). Consequentialism is often contrasted with 'deontological' ethics, as if these two kinds of moral theory divided the entire field between them. This is certainly not correct. There exist other possibilities (as we shall see in later chapters). But deontological ethics and consequentialist ethics do differ in a very radical manner: according to deontological ethics it is the nature of the act as such that is decisive to its moral status. If consequentialism invites us to consider the consequences of the act, deontological ethics invites us to consider the act without pondering its consequences.

The roots of the word 'deontology' can be found in the Greek words *deon*, duty, and *logos*, science. The best-known representative of deontological ethics is the German philosopher Immanuel Kant. According to deontological ethics, some types of actions are prohibited, or obligatory, irrespective of their consequences. In this chapter I will make only a very rough representation of Kant's moral philosophy. Rather than discuss his entire moral philosophy, I will try to find at least a few absolute moral prohibitions and injunctions defended by him, and by many other thinkers as well, in order to find out whether it would be reasonable to abide by them.

Kantianism

Kantianism is sometimes identified with an idea put forward by Kant to the effect that the only thing that is good in all circumstances is good will. This is how he puts the point in his enormously influential book *Groundwork* (1785):

> It is impossible to think of anything at all in the world, or indeed even beyond it that could be considered good without limitation except a good will. (*Groundwork*, p. 7)

Note, however, that this idea is not 'deontological' in the sense described here. It does not focus our attention on the act itself. It does not define a class of right actions, or wrong actions, or obligatory actions at all. As a matter of fact, it represents a line of thought that will be discussed more thoroughly in Chapter 6 which considers virtue ethics. The truth about Kant is that he holds an ethical theory with two very different tenets. The first is the one expressed in the quotation above. The other is his deontology, his idea that some actions are right or obligatory irrespective of their consequences, while other actions are wrong irrespective of their consequences.

How these two tenets of his moral thinking fit together is problematic. From Kant's point of view, it is fine if an obligatory action is performed for the right motive (good will), of course, but what can he say of obligatory actions performed for the wrong motive, or wrong actions performed for the right motive? The moral status of such actions seems to me a little vague in Kant's moral philosophy, but I will not discuss this any further in the present context (I will return to a similar problem when discussing virtue ethics, however). Here the focus will be exclusively on the deontological aspect of Kant's moral philosophy. The focus will be on actions proclaimed by Kant to be absolutely wrong and, in particular, on one such type of action: the deliberate and active killing of innocent human beings. If anything is absolutely wrong, it would appear that this is it.

Kant thought that there exists one very general 'perfect' duty which is absolute, categorical and such that reason alone dictates it to any rational human being. He speaks of this duty as the categorical imperative and states it as follows:

> There is, therefore, only a single categorical imperative and it is this: *act only in accordance with that maxim through which you can at*

the same time will that it become a universal law. (*Groundwork*,
p. 31, emphasis in the original)

Why does Kant state this basic moral principle as an imperative?
Why does he not state it as follows: *an action is right if and only
if it is in accordance with a maxim which the agent can will that
it should become a universal law?* And what does he mean by
calling this imperative 'categorical'?

The second question is most easily dealt with. By calling
the imperative 'categorical', Kant wants to contrast it with im-
peratives that are 'conditional'. A conditional imperative is an
imperative such as the following one: 'If you want to find the best
way from St Petersburg to Kaliningrad, use a modern map!' This
imperative is really an empirical statement in disguise. It has no
normative force for a person who has no interest in finding the
way from St Petersburg to Kaliningrad. It informs us about a
factual relation between a certain goal and certain means to
achieve it. A categorical imperative, in contrast, is thought to
have a binding force for any person, irrespective of his or her
interests and inclinations.

The first question about why Kant formulates his basic moral
principle as he does is more complicated. The right answer to it
must account for several different strands in Kant's moral
metaethics: on the one hand, his belief that moral principles are
commands, on the other hand, his belief that moral principles
have truth-values and, finally, his belief that, although moral
principles are a kind of command, there is no one (such as God
or nature) issuing them to us; any rational agent must just find
that they are binding on him or her.

These strands are not easily reconciled, but it would take us
deeply into metaethics to try to sort them out. I will simply
assume that Kant's categorical imperative is equivalent to a moral
principle stated in the indicative mood, and thus that Kant's categorical imperative is in competition with egoism, utilitarianism
and other moral theories.

Kant formulates his categorical imperative in various ways.
Here is another formulation:

*So act that you use humanity, whether in your own person or in the
person of any other, always at the same time as an end, never merely
as a means.* (*Groundwork*, p. 38, emphasis in the original)

Kant seems to have thought that these and other formulations are equivalent. But it is hard to follow him on this point. And from the categorical imperative he 'deduces' all sorts of moral duties, like, for instance, that it is always wrong to tell a lie, to kill, to commit suicide or to break a promise. All this is hard to digest. It is difficult to understand how he can believe that the different formulations of the categorical imperative can be equivalent, and it is hard to follow his argument when he 'deduces' different duties from the imperative. The original formulation of the imperative, on which I will focus exclusively, is well in line with a standard moral argument, however. I am thinking of a line of argument we have all at some time used: What would happen if everyone did that? we have asked rhetorically. If what would happen would be bad or unthinkable, then, it is assumed, that is a reason to abstain from the action in question.

Note that this line of argument is in a way very similar to what we have called in a previous chapter 'rule' utilitarianism. However, there are both similarities and differences between Kant's categorical imperative and rule utilitarianism. One difference is the following. According to rule utilitarianism, bad consequences of general conformance with a rule mean bad consequences from the point of view of welfare. Kant will have none of this. When he speaks of a maxim such that we cannot will that it becomes a universal law, the paradigmatic example is something like the following. Suppose I ponder whether I should tell a lie. I then ask myself: can I will that telling lies becomes a universal law? I realise that I cannot will this. Why? Because if everyone were to tell lies all the time, communication would break down. It would be impossible not only to tell lies, but to tell the truth as well. So I have an absolute (perfect) duty never to tell a lie.

A similarity between Kant's categorical imperative and rule utilitarianism is a fundamental vagueness in both approaches. To each action, according to Kant, there exists a corresponding maxim. In a similar vein, to each action there corresponds, according to rule utilitarianism, a certain rule. Which maxim? Which rule? We are invited to contemplate what would happen if everyone were to do *the same*. But when are two actions *the same*? We need some criterion of sameness, and neither Kant nor the rule utilitarian has ever provided us with one. If I contemplate whether I should tell a lie in order not to hurt someone who is near and dear to me, is then 'telling a lie' a reasonable ground for generalisation? Or should I try to find out the consequences of 'everyone telling lies in situations where the truth would hurt someone who is near and dear to them'? Or is the proper kind of action to consider: 'lies told in situations where this maximises the sum total of welfare'? It is obvious that according to the latter interpretation rule utilitarianism collapses into ordinary 'act' utilitarianism of the kind we know from Chapter 2. Kant would not accept this kind of generalisation, of course, but it is not clear exactly what kind of generalisation he is after. Before we have stipulated how we can find the relevant 'maxim' behind particular actions there is no way for us to evaluate the categorical imperative. But this does not mean that there are no absolute duties.

Even if Kant has not arrived at absolute duties in any impeccable way, he may have hit on a crucial moral truth. He may be right in his insistence that, in addition to a class of less strict, 'imperfect' duties (such as the duty to help each other), there exists a class of absolute moral duties (such as the duty never to kill an innocent human being). This seems to be Kant's view. Is he right about this? Are there absolute duties? Are there certain kinds of actions that we can clearly define such that we ought to perform, or not perform, irrespective of their consequences in the individual case?

Let us leave Kant to one side and ponder whether there are such actions. And let us leave behind those putative examples suggested by Kant that may strike a modern reader as rather moralistic, such as the absolute rule that one should never tell a lie or break a promise. Let us instead concentrate on the absolute prohibition against murder, which seems to be the most plausible example in a list of absolute duties, and also on the corresponding putative duty to execute those who have violated this prohibition. Is it true that it is always wrong to kill? Is it mandatory, if possible, to convict and execute those who have violated this prohibition? I will discuss these questions in order.

Thou shalt not kill!

The idea that killing is absolutely forbidden is not exclusive to Kant, of course. In many religions this idea is given some kind of defence, and, in its religious form, we know the rule not to kill as the 'sanctity of life' doctrine. However, the doctrine has rarely been defended in any simple form. Not all kinds of killing are forbidden, according to the sanctity of life doctrine or according to Kant. Kant did not object to the killing of animals. It is the killing of *human beings* that has been considered wrong. But even this prohibition needs qualification: according to Kant we ought to execute murderers. So it is really only the killing of *innocent* human beings that has been considered to be absolutely wrong.

Is Kant right about this? Is, in this manner, the innocent human life sacred? Is it always wrong to kill an innocent human being, even if, for example, by killing one we may save three? Remember Philippa Foot's trolley case. Is it wrong to flick the switch? Is it wrong to kill innocent human beings even at their own request, for example in order to bring an end to suffering at the very end of their lives (euthanasia)?

Many seem to share Kant's view and adopt the sanctity of life doctrine. However, in order to make the view that it is always wrong to kill innocent human beings as plausible as possible, we must qualify it further. In particular, we must find a version allowing us to flick the switch in the original trolley example. I will do so with the help of some distinctions often made in the discussion of euthanasia.

Euthanasia

In the Netherlands and in Belgium it is permissible for a person suffering from an incurable disease and who wants to be spared living out the remainder of his or her life to request a doctor to end his or her life. And in the state of Oregon, a patient in similar circumstances can procure assistance from a doctor if he or she decides to commit suicide. However, in most countries this is totally out of question. Why is this so? A possible explanation may be that these systems violate the basic moral rule that it is always wrong to kill an innocent human being, and that this rule has strong support, at least among politicians and physicians.

However, even in countries where euthanasia and medically assisted suicide are strongly prohibited, patients suffering from incurable diseases are sometimes spared having to live out the rest of their lives. The means used in these cases are either *passive* or such that there is no *intention* on the part of the doctor to shorten the patient's life. Both these distinctions, between active and passive killing and intentional and unintentional killing, have been important in the discussion about the sanctity of life doctrine. Let me explain in some detail how we are to understand them.

Take, first, the distinction between acts and omissions. On this idea, while it is always wrong actively to kill a person, it may sometimes be right to allow death to come about through natural means. Active killing is always wrong, but what we may call 'passive' killing or 'allowing' a patient to die may sometimes be right.

Is the distinction between active and passive killing at all comprehensible? It is true that the distinction between acts and omissions does not allow us to say, in relation to concrete and particular actions, whether they fall into either the active or the passive category, or so I am prepared to argue. Each concrete action can be described in some way which makes it active. For example, not to help a person who is drowning can be described as *actively turning a blind eye to what is happening*. However, some *kinds* of actions (some action types) allow that we sort instances (tokens) of them into the active or passive category. To *help* a person is an example of this. We can actively help people, but we can also help people passively by merely allowing benefits to befall them. And killing is indeed an example of this. There are clear-cut cases of active killing and there are clear-cut cases of passive killing (of allowing nature to take its course). No criterion can be formulated here, I submit, but no criterion is really needed. Our linguistic intuitions are clear enough. In particular cases we can say of an act of killing whether it is active or passive, even if we cannot always state our reasons for the classification in a completely general form. Not to feed a patient who, in consequence, starves to death is to kill passively, while injecting an opioid that kills the patient is to kill actively.

Let us now consider the distinction between different intentions behind the (active or passive) killing of a patient. The distinction is made in relation to what has been called the principle of 'double effect'. According to this principle, it is always wrong intentionally to kill a patient, but it may be right to provide aggressive palliative care with the intention of relieving pain, even if it can be foreseen that the patient will die from the care in question. This may be right provided that, in the circumstances, it is a good thing to have the patient free of pain, and provided that there is some reasonable proportion between the (first) good effect (the patient being free of pain) and the (second) bad effect (death being somewhat hastened), and provided the death of the patient is not sought as a means of achieving the good effect.

Is the principle comprehensible? Certainly, it may be very difficult to tell whether a specific doctor in a specific situation, by administering opioids in a manner that hastens death, does or does not intend the death of a patient. This may be difficult to tell even for the doctor him- or herself. *In principle*, however, there is a clear difference between a case where the doctor gives the medication with the intention of killing the patient, because this is considered the best way to relieve the patient's pain, and, on the other hand, a case where the doctor administers the medication in order to relieve pain (realising that the patient may die as an unwanted but unavoidable consequence of the medication).

A way of checking whether, according to this principle, the intention of the doctor is the right one is to ask the doctor: 'If you could have relieved pain in another way that would not have hastened death, would you have done so?'

The role of the principles

Which roles do the distinctions between active and passive killing and the principle of double effect play in standard moral thinking? It may seem that they play no role whatever. For not only in the Netherlands and Belgium, but in most other countries as well, both active killing of patients and intentional killing of patients take place. When a patient is given a painkilling injection that not only kills the pain but the patient as well, the killing of the patient is certainly active. And when the doctor stops feeding a patient who is in a persistent vegetative state, then the intention is to allow the patient to die. However, the combination of active and intentional killing is strictly prohibited in most countries. The legal and (official) moral situation can be represented in these countries as seen in Figure 4.1.

This may seem very strange. If active killing is allowed and if intentional killing is allowed, what is so problematic about their combination? It seems to me that a defensible answer to this question could be as follows. While it is not morally problematic

Killing	Death intended	Death merely foreseen
Active	FORBIDDEN	TOLERATED
Passive	TOLERATED	TOLERATED

Figure 4.1 Four ways of shortening life

as such to kill passively (to allow nature to take its course), it is morally problematic as such to kill actively. This does not mean, of course, that *all* instances of passive killing are morally acceptable. Sometimes it *is* morally wrong to kill passively. As a matter of fact it is wrong – very wrong – in most cases. But when it is wrong to kill passively, this is not due to any *inherent* wrongness in the act, but due to particular *consequences* of the act, or due to the fact that some rights of the patient have been violated. It may, for example, be wrong to allow a patient to die because of lack of treatment if one has promised, or undertaken, to provide the treatment in question, and most obviously if the treatment would have saved the patient. This may even be seriously wrong. However, the wrongness is not inherent in the act itself, which is an act of passive, not active, killing.

But to condemn all kinds of active killing, irrespective of the consequences, may be to go too far, even when we restrict it to innocent human beings. Here a further qualification may be needed if we want to make the sanctity of life doctrine as plausible as possible. We can make the distinction with reference to the principle of double effect. What is *inherently* wrong is only active killing *with the intention to kill* (actively). If the killing is active, but death merely a foreseen and not intended consequence of the act in question, then the action may be right. At least it is not inherently wrong. If it is beneficial to the patient, and if certain other criteria are satisfied, it may even be morally permissible or mandatory. However, actively and deliberately to kill a patient is wrong, period; that is, it is wrong irrespective of the consequences. This is the hard core of the (deontological) sanctity of life doctrine.

A reasonable conjecture is that some thinking along these lines must lie behind the widespread prohibition against active and intentional killing of patients at their request (euthanasia), while palliative care that hastens death, as well as the withdrawal of treatment and hydration with the intention of hastening death, is accepted. And it seems to me that this is also the most plausible version of the sanctity of life doctrine. With respect to the trolley cases, this line of argument indicates that it is right to flick the switch in the original case, since the killing of the person on the side-track in the Switch case is not intentional, but that it is wrong to push the big man onto the track in the Footbridge case. This fits well with how people usually judge the cases. However, according to this line of reasoning, at variance with how people often judge the cases, it is wrong to flick the switch in the modified version of the example, the Loop case, where a person tied to the track is used as a means to stop the trolley.

But is the doctrine acceptable even in its most plausible form? Before I address this question, allow me to discuss one more example, besides euthanasia, where some people are actively and deliberately killed. I am thinking of a case similar to the trolley one, where this is done in order to save lives.

The survival lottery

Consider the following problem. A broadcasting company is casting a reality TV show. The intention is to transport sixteen people, together with the host of the show, to a small island in the Pacific Ocean. The members of the expedition will gather for successive tribal councils and cast their votes. One by one the members of the expedition will be voted off the island. Whoever is eventually left at the end of the show with the host is the 'Survivor' and wins a fortune.

On their way to the island, however, the plane they are travelling in develops a technical problem. After an emergency landing on the water in the middle of nowhere the aeroplane soon sinks, taking the crew with it into deep water. The members of the expedition, together with the host of the show, however, succeed in swimming to a nearby island. Here they find themselves on wasteland. They possess one sharp knife and functioning lighter, they find a well which provides them with fresh water, they can make up a fire using driftwood which they collect on the shore, but there is nothing for them to eat: no fish, no game, no roots or vegetables. They wait for help but none arrives. After two weeks they realise that they will all probably starve to death. They gather for their first tribal council and agree to run a survival lottery. The 'winner' of the lottery will be held down by the rest, killed with the sharp knife, roasted over the fire and then consumed. One person a week will be killed in accordance with the rules of the lottery. Two members of the expedition declare that they are Kantians. They are not willing to take part in the lottery, and this is accepted by the rest. After several weeks five have been killed and eaten (among them the host of the show, who was the third to draw the killing ticket in the lottery). The two Kantians have meanwhile died from starvation and have been buried according to their wishes. Then a ship arrives and the nine survivors are rescued.

According to utilitarianism, the survivors have probably acted rightly. What better option was there? In this assessment the egoist will concur, of course. And both utilitarians and contractual egoists, who want in general to uphold a strong ban on murder in order to feel safe in society, may, considering the fact that the lottery was fair and the Kantians were spared, allow that, in this case, no punishment should be meted out. The situation was exceptional, so there is no point in prosecuting the survivors. On the contrary, a utilitarian or ethical egoist may even admire their wise decision and congratulate them on their good luck. According to the sanctity of life doctrine, however, the survivors have acted wrongly. They are mass murderers who deserve just punishment.

Just punishment

What, then, according to deontological ethics, does just punishment amount to? Utilitarians and egoists of the contractual variety want a system of punishments designed so that everyone can feel a maximum of security. This means that the system of criminal justice should prevent people from committing crimes by threatening them with those kinds of punishment that are best suited to the aim of preventing further crime. At the same time, those who do not commit crimes should feel reasonably certain that they will not be punished. The system is consistently looking forwards.

The goal of the system of punishment is very different, according to deontological ethics. When a person commits a crime this means, according to deontologists, that he or she becomes afflicted with *guilt*. And a guilty person *deserves* to be punished.

The punishment should be given as an act of respect for the criminal, not for any reasons of expediency. If the system of punishment has a deterrent effect, then this is a 'second', double effect of the system. Those who have constructed the system may gratefully acknowledge this effect, but it must not be sought. The system should be consistently looking backwards.

The utilitarian or egoistic defence of a system of punishment does not require that people have 'free will'; at least it is not required that free will exists in any deep 'philosophical' sense. It is enough, according to these views, that the existence of a system of punishment can make people behave more decently in relation to each other. The deontological system of punishment, however, places a heavy burden on the notion of free will. Unless the perpetrator of a specific criminal action was free to avoid committing it, it would not be fair to punish him or her. However, if the perpetrator was free to act otherwise, but chose to do evil, then the punishment is justified. Society owes the punishment to the perpetrator.

The most serious moral mistake a human being can make, as we have seen, according to both Kant's deontological ethics and to the sanctity of life doctrine, is intentionally and actively killing an innocent human being. What is the appropriate punishment for this crime? What kind of punishment is it that we owe the murderer?

Kant did not hesitate in answering this question. A person who is guilty of murder deserves to die. Kant would have advised that the survivors of the lottery described above be executed!

Capital punishment

For a utilitarian or an ethical egoist pondering what kind of social contract to construct, the question of capital punishment is a pragmatic one. Utilitarians and ethical egoists do not adopt a principled stance on capital punishment. If they become convinced that a system of capital punishment offers a maximum of security in society, then they will defend it, otherwise not.

Or could it be argued that capital punishment is so cruel and unusual that a utilitarian must at least object to it on that ground? This is hard to accept. The killing of a person convicted of murder can take a form similar to euthanasia. In which case it is not cruel for there is nothing unusual in murderers having to wait for their execution. Suddenly they know that they have only a short time left to live. But the same is true of a person who suddenly catches a terminal disease. Such patients often ask themselves: 'Why did this happen to me?' Convicts on death row have one advantage over them: they know the answer.

So, in sum, there seems to exist no reasons to conclude that capital punishment is so cruel or unusual that it must, for that reason, be rejected by a utilitarian. Indeed, some utilitarians, such as J. S. Mill, have argued from reasons of humanity in defence of capital punishment, believing that long terms of imprisonment harm the murderer more than death.

I think it clear that if they become convinced that capital punishment in terms of its deterrent effect is better than long prison sentences, then not only ethical egoists but utilitarians too must come to accept it. A system of capital punishment that is an active deterrent against murder will, egoists and utilitarians alike must argue, render life more secure. The utilitarians, concerned also for the welfare of perpetrators, will add that if capital punishment has a deterrent effect, those who are deterred from committing murder are also spared the sad fate of becoming murderers.

But if this is so, how can it be explained that so many utilitarians have argued against capital punishment? The reason is that they have doubted that the deterrent effect of capital punishment is better than long prison sentences. They have cited empirical evidence to this effect and have found reasons to believe that, in some circumstances, a system of capital punishment may engender, rather than deter, murder. Think of those people who know that if arrested they will be convicted of murder and executed. They will have no reason whatever not to kill in order to get away with what they have already done.

But note that neither the utilitarians nor the ethical egoists are principled in their rejection of capital punishment when they reject it. And some of them defend it, making other empirical assumptions than the ones referred to here.

The situation is very different for the adherents of deontological ethics. According to them, there is an intimate relation between wrongdoing, guilt and deserved punishment. The perpetrator who is guilty of wrongdoing deserves his or her punishment. Society owes the punishment to the criminal because of the crime committed. The purpose of the punishment is not future improvement of either society or the criminal. The rationale behind the punishment can be found in the past, in the deed committed by the perpetrator. This is how Kant writes about this in his *Rechtslehre* (1797):

> Judicial punishment can never be used merely as a means to promote some other good for the criminal himself or for civil society, but instead it must in all cases be imposed on him only on the ground that he has committed a crime. (*Metaphysical Elements of Justice*, p. 138)

The same argument applies to capital punishment. This is how Kant writes about this:

> Even if a civil society were to dissolve itself by common agreement of all its members (for example, if the people inhabiting an island decided to separate and disperse themselves around the world), the last murderer remaining in prison must first be executed, so that everyone will duly receive what his actions are worth and so that the bloodguilt thereof will not be fixed on the people because they failed to insist on carrying out the punishment; for if they fail to do so, they may be regarded as accomplices in this public violation of legal justice. (Ibid., p. 140)

Capital punishment can be seen as the expression of the utmost reverence for the sanctity of life. It is also an expression of *lex talionis*, or an eye for an eye. However, those who find this too cruel may argue, of course, that human life, innocent or not, is so sacred that even the execution of a murderer is an act of murder. The Vatican used to argue, following Thomas Aquinas, and in accordance with the view put forward by Kant, that murderers deserve to be executed. Now, however, the Vatican has adopted the latter stance and campaigns for the abolition of capital punishment.

Should we accept the sanctity of life doctrine?

We have learnt something about the consequences of applying the sanctity of life doctrine to different kinds of actions, and we have considered the sanctity of life doctrine to be the most plausible part of deontological ethics. Is the doctrine plausible?

We saw with respect to suicide and euthanasia that the view does prohibit both practices, which some people may find cruel. However, the doctrine is more flexible than at first meets the eye. It does allow people who are suffering from an incurable and terminal disease to be spared their suffering. This can be achieved by both active means and means where death is sought intentionally, provided only that death is not both actively and intentionally brought about. From a utilitarian or egoist point of view this may be criticised as a kind of hypocrisy, of course. Why not allow the doctor to kill the patient, once it has been decided that life has no more to offer the patient in terms of quality of life? Why *deny* the patient this service, if it is what the patient wants? However, the adherent of the sanctity of life doctrine will not accept that the practice involves any hypocrisy. It gives the patient *almost* everything the patient asks for and it means that the doctor does *everything* he or she can do for the patient, without acting immorally.

But *why* is it wrong actively and intentionally to kill a human being when this is in the best interest of the human being who requests it? It is hard to see that any reference to Kant's categorical imperative can help us to this conclusion. In fact, there does not seem to exist any knockdown argument in defence of deontological ethics. But this is true of utilitarianism and egoism as well.

However, each theory faces some hard cases. Euthanasia is perhaps not the worst case for deontological ethics. The survival lottery may be thought to provide us with a more problematic case. Here deontological ethics in general, and the sanctity of life doctrine in particular, lead us to the conclusion that the survivors are murderers. Can this really be an acceptable conclusion?

To be sure, the adherent of utilitarianism or egoism would argue, if some people do not want to take part in a survival lottery, they should be assured that no one will force them. And it would be reasonable to punish anyone who had forced a Kantian into such a lottery. But in the example we discussed, the Kantians were exempted from the lottery. So what wrong has been committed? Should not the Kantians, who do not want to take part in the lottery, at least tolerate it among those who consent? Why not tolerate a practice when otherwise all, rather than a few, will lose their lives?

Consider the case of abortion. It is reasonable to claim that the foetus is a human being (a human organism). It is also reasonable to claim that the foetus is innocent. But then abortion, no matter how early in the pregnancy it takes place, is as serious a moral crime as murder, according to deontological ethics. This is a very strict view of abortion: abortion is as serious a crime as murder. But surely this argument can be made to work the other way round as well: murder is no more serious than abortion. It is obvious that people have conflicting intuitions with respect to abortion. Some find that the sanctity of life doctrine is most urgently needed in the discussion about abortion, since it is the only moral stance that unequivocally gives the right answer: abortion is wrong. Others may find that at last we have found a clear *reductio ad absurdum* of the sanctity of life doctrine.

What are we finally to say of the retributivism associated with deontological ethics? Is it true that we owe the punishment to the criminal? Can a criminal ever 'deserve' capital punishment?

There are some difficult metaphysical problems with this. We have seen that the view presupposes that we have, in ordinary circumstances, 'free will'. Is it true that we have such a thing as free will? There is no unanimity about this among those who have thought hard about the question. Even Kant had to admit that he made the assumption that we have free will, not because he saw any conclusive reason to this effect, but because the assumption was needed in his version of deontological ethics.

A utilitarian will find the retributivist view of punishment primitively atavistic, of course. According to the retributive view, a criminal should be punished even if, from a preventive point of view, there is no point in the punishment. But in that case, the utilitarian would ask, why cause *unnecessary* pain to a criminal? There is no point in a system of punishment which has no deterrent effect. However, the adherent of retributivist deontological ethics has an answer to this question. The pain inflicted through punishment, even if it does not deter from further crime, is far from unnecessary. From a moral point of view, this is necessary pain.

Assume for a moment that the retributivist is right. What kind of punishment would be appropriate for murder? Should the retributivist accept capital punishment?

I think the retributivist faces a genuine dilemma here. While the utilitarian or ethical egoist can adopt a pragmatic stance to capital punishment, accepting it if it tends to have good effects and otherwise rejecting it, the deontological retributivist seems to be trapped in either of two very extreme views. The retributivist will have to argue either that murderers should always be executed, even when this means no gain from the point of view of deterrence, or that they should never be executed, even when this means that we can save innocent human lives.

The former view, which used to be the view of the Roman Catholic Church, strikes me as cruel, while the latter, which has now been adopted by the Vatican, strikes me as squeamish. But by saying so, I am just expressing my own moral intuitions.

Further reading about deontological ethics

Kant's *Groundwork of the Metaphysics of Morals*, translated and edited by Mary Gregor with an introduction by Christine M. Korsgaard (Cambridge: Cambridge University Press, 1998) has here been quoted. Good introductions to Kant are Christine Korsgaard's *The Kingdom of Ends* (New York: Cambridge University Press, 1996) and Onora Nells' (now O'Neill) classic *Acting on Principle: An Essay on Kantian Ethics* (New York and London: Columbia University Press, 1975). On the distinction between acts and omissions, see Jonathan Bennett, *The Act Itself* (Oxford: Oxford University Press, 1995) and A. Donagan, *The Theory of Morality* (Chicago: The University of Chicago Press, 1977). The moral relevance of the active/passive distinction is criticised by James Rachels in 'Active and Passive Euthanasia', *New England Journal of Medicine*, 292, 2, 1975, pp. 78–80. However, the validity of his argument has been questioned by Shelly Kagan ('The Additive Fallacy', *Ethics*, 1988, pp. 5–31). An authoritative statement of the principle of double effect can be found in *New Catholic Encyclopedia* (New York: McGraw-Hill, 1967). See also P. A. Woodward (ed.), *The Doctrine of Double Effect: Philosophers Debate a Controversial Moral Principle* (Notre Dame, IN: University of Notre Dame Press, 2001). A version of the survival lottery is discussed in John Harris, *The Value of Life* (London: Routledge, 1985). The well-known quotations from Kant on crime and punishment are here taken from *Metaphysical Elements of Justice*, 2nd edn, translated with introduction and notes by John Ladd (Indianapolis: Hackett, 1999). Critical discussions of the sanctity of life doctrine can be found in Helga Kuhse, *The Sanctity-of-Life Doctrine in Medicine: A Critique* (Oxford: Clarendon Press, 1987) and in Peter Singer, *Rethinking Life and Death* (New York: St. Martin's Press, 1995).

5

Moral Rights

Introduction

According to deontological ethics, as presented by Kant, there are absolute duties binding all human beings without any further motivation. Being rational beings, we can understand that these duties exist. Even utilitarians and ethical egoists believe in duties, we have seen, but in these moral traditions the duties originate in the consequences of our actions with respect to welfare. There exists a third idea of the origin of moral duties: the moral rights tradition. According to this tradition there exist absolute moral duties arising from absolute moral rights. We possess these absolute moral rights simply because we are the kind of creatures we are. We all have a duty to respect these moral rights. These rights appear to agents as a 'side-constraint' on what we are allowed to do. I shall now discuss this tradition in detail.

The point of departure of the moral rights tradition is the idea that each moral subject has a right to a kind of moral integrity. This right is absolute; it arises from the fact that each moral subject 'owns', in a moral sense, him- or herself, and it is not derived from any other kind of consideration. We who have such rights have them just because we are the kind of creatures we are. This is what gives us self-ownership and hence our moral standing.

Note that we are speaking here of moral rights that exist irrespective of whether they are safeguarded by law. Even if the law allows me to violate a moral right of yours, it would be morally wrong for me to do so. Even in a state of nature these rights exist and should be respected. And even if, in a democracy, there exists a certain law exhorting me to violate some of your

73

rights, I must not do so. If I do, then my action is immoral. In cases where morality and the law are in conflict, we ought to obey the moral law rather than the positive law. And the conflict should urgently be resolved by legal reform.

It is only natural that the moral rights tradition has appeared in tandem with moral contractualism. When it does, the moral contract that is sanctioned is different from the one discussed in the chapter on ethical egoism. According to Hobbes and the ethical egoists, when rational people make up their social contract they bargain without taking any moral concern whatever. They are free to threaten to kill each other in order to improve their terms. The contract they arrive at therefore reflects their respective strengths. The social contract presupposed by the moral rights tradition is very different. Here people are supposed to bargain too, but in doing so they must respect each other's moral rights.

But even from such a narrow point of departure there is much room for improvement of the lot of everyone, of course. In particular, there is room for a minimal 'night watchman' state, which ensures that contracts are followed and no rights are violated.

Enough has been said about contractualism (in Chapter 2), however, so I will say no more about it in the present context. Instead, I will focus on the issue of moral rights.

Rights

What does it mean for a person to have a moral 'right' to something? And what is it that one can have a moral right to? In the tradition we are discussing, what we have a right to can be conceived of as a 'thing', and I will use the variable X to represent things of this nature. This allows us to say that my having a right to X involves two things. First of all, if I have a moral right to X, then I have a guarantee that when I use X as I see fit I am not acting wrongly – to the extent that I do not use X to violate the rights of any one else. Second, if I have a moral right to X, then if someone stops me from using X as I see fit – again provided I do not violate any moral rights – this person is acting wrongly.

Note once again that we are here speaking of 'right' and 'wrong' in a *moral* sense. This means that if I have a moral right to X and use X as I see fit, then my action is *morally* permitted (right). If you try to stop me, you commit a *moral* mistake. Once again, this is true provided I do not use X to violate the rights of any one else.

Can a utilitarian accept that there are moral rights of this kind? It is hard to believe that there exists any X such that whenever an agent uses X as he or she sees fit, the sum total of welfare is maximised. The very point in granting the individual rights, in the way the moral rights tradition does, is to allow the individual some moral 'space'. But utilitarians sometimes support such things as the UN Charter of Human Rights. How is this possible? The explanation is that utilitarians sometimes accept moral rights in a derived sense. When a utilitarian says, for example, that each human being has a right to life, this means that there exists a robust defence of the claim that it would be a good idea (on the whole) to have an act of law prohibiting the (arbitrary) killing of human beings.

This is, for example, what J. S. Mill has to say about rights:

> When we call anything a person's right, we mean that he has a valid claim on society to protect him in the possession of it, either by the force of law, or by that of education and opinion ... To have a right, then, is, I conceive, to have something which society ought to defend me in the possession of. If the objector goes on to ask, why it ought? I can give him no other reason than general utility. ('Utilitarianism', p. 309)

Note that such a right may exist even if no law (yet) exists to safeguard it. However, note also that, according to this view, the existence of such a (utilitarian) right is hardly an *argument* why a law should be enacted protecting it. It is rather itself the *conclusion* of such an argument.

As an historical aside it should be noted that Bentham did not believe in derived rights of this kind. He attacked the human rights declaration put forward by the French revolutionaries. Natural rights are 'nonsense', he claimed, and imprescriptible rights 'nonsense upon stilts'. Why did he not believe at least in derived individual rights? He did not believe that any stable rationale existed for any rights that could be 'specifically described'.

The point of departure of the moral rights tradition has been some idea of *natural* rights. Even if this is established terminology I am not very happy with it. The term 'natural rights' suggests both that rights of the kind we are discussing here exist (which is perfectly in order) and that these rights are somehow part of the fabric of nature itself. The latter aspect has to do with metaethics and not with normative ethics, and it is not a good idea to conflate the two. A person who doubts the metaethical (onto-logical) idea that moral rights exist in nature, independently of our conceptualisation, may still endorse the idea that some notion of moral rights is the fundamental point of departure in a sound moral argument. And those who deny that moral rights can provide us with premises of sound moral arguments may still believe in moral realism. I will therefore avoid speaking of 'natural rights' and speak instead simply of moral rights.

The moral rights tradition has its roots in antiquity, with the Greek Stoic philosopher Chrysippus (*c.* 280–*c.* 205) as its most famous advocate. The tradition was taken up again during the Renaissance by the Dutch thinker Hugo Grotius (1583–1645) and was given authoritative statement by the English philosopher John Locke (1632–1704). Today we know the tradition first and foremost through a radical and enormously influential defence of the concept put forward by the Harvard philosopher Robert Nozick in *Anarchy, State, and Utopia* (1974). In this chapter I will focus on Nozick's timely and radical version of the moral rights tradition, but give some comments on Locke's version as well.

Moral subjects

According to the moral rights tradition in general, there exist moral subjects who have moral rights by virtue of being the kind of creatures they are. Such moral subjects have certain rights, first and foremost to their own bodies, their own talents, and so forth. They 'own' themselves. These things constitute their *suum*, to use the Latin term. This *suum* can be extended when the individual acquires property, in a way to be described in the next section.

Who are the possessors of moral rights? What does it mean to be a moral subject? There is no unanimity among the adherents of the moral rights tradition when they attempt to answer these questions, and there exists a long history of sexist prejudices in this area. Traditionally, only adult men were considered full moral subjects. I will say no more of this, however. Here I am searching for a version of the moral rights theory which makes it as plausible as possible.

Some kind of reference to a capacity to function as a moral agent has often been made when it has been specified what it means to be a moral subject. A moral subject is an autonomous moral *agent*, a *person*, someone who can make *choices* and view him- or herself as *responsible* for the consequences of his or her actions; these are only examples of the way the notion of a moral subject has been delineated. I will return to this question below, since the exact answer seems to have important bearings on the plausibility of the moral rights theory as such.

How do we acquire moral rights?

Each individual has a right to, or owns, him- or herself. This is the hard core of the moral rights tradition. But the tradition does not stop at self-ownership. We can also acquire rights to individual property. The way to acquire property is to be the first to get hold of it. According to Locke, we all used to own the commons together. They had been given to us by God. However, each individual could acquire what he or she saw fit from the commons by, for example, mixing his or her labour with the soil. Such an acquisition is just, provided that there is 'enough and as good left in common for others'. Nozick has called this latter clause 'Locke's proviso'.

Note, however, that it is far from clear how this proviso should be interpreted in detail. Let us just note in the present context that, according to Nozick, the crucial thing is that *others are not made worse off* by my just, original acquisition of something. It is also an open question *how much* of the soil I can make part of my original acquisition. Do I have to handle it in order to make it mine? Should I erect a fence around it? Is it enough if I simply lay eyes on it?

Whatever you have originally acquired, in a proper fashion, is yours. You have a moral right to it. This means, we recall, that by doing whatever you see fit with it, provided you do not violate any rights, you are acting rightly. And if anyone were to stop you from doing this, this person would be acting wrongly.

At least this is how Nozick interprets the theory. Whatever I have acquired a right to I can use as I see fit. Suppose I own an axe. I can give it away, I can use it for productive ends or I can destroy it. But I cannot cleave your head with it. That would be to violate your right to your head (and your life).

Note that Nozick's point of departure is very different from Locke's. Locke believes that God has given the commons to us. We own them together. According to Nozick's secular version of the theory, no one owns the commons. Note also that while Locke wanted to defend the individual against the sovereign, supposed to have divine authority over his or her subjects, Nozick wants to protect the individual from interference from other individuals. This can explain some other differences between their theories.

They both argue that we are free to use our property as we see fit, so long as we do not violate the rights of others. However, while Nozick argues that we can only violate the rights of others if actively and deliberately we take their property from them or invade their privacy, Locke believed that people also had certain rights to aid from others, and property owners, according to Locke, were not free to destroy their property. This brings Locke's thinking closer to utilitarianism than Nozick's.

This is what Locke himself says about his proviso:

> It will perhaps be objected to this, That if gathering the Acorns, or other Fruits of the Earth ... makes a right to them, then any one may ingrossas much as he will. To which I Answer, Not so. The same Law of Nature, that does by this means give us Property, does also *bound that Property* too. *God has given us all things richly* ... But how far has he given it us? To enjoy. As much as any one can make use of to any advantage of life before it spoils: so much he may by his labour fix a Property in. Whatever is beyond this, is more than his share, and belongs to others. Nothing was made by God for Man to spoil or destroy. (*Two Treatises of Government*, II:31)

Locke also states explicitly that there exists a right to charity:

> Charity gives every Man a Title to so much out of another's Plenty, as will keep him from extream want, where he has no means to subsist otherwise. (Ibid., I:42)

Nozick does not quote passages such as these from Locke, and the reason he does not, I suppose, is that he does not want to accept them. His version of the moral rights theory does not allow for 'positive' rights of the kind here defined. And I will focus on Nozick's interpretation of the theory. After all, it gives us a more startling alternative to other moral theories in general, and to utilitarianism in particular. According to Nozick, we have no moral obligation to share our property with those who need it. But we are allowed to do so, of course, even according to Nozick; he may also admit that it would be *noble* of us if we did.

We have seen that each moral subject owns him- or herself and the property he or she has acquired in the right way (respecting the proviso). To this should be added a right to give property away as one sees fit. This prepares for yet another way to acquire property. We can receive it as a gift or in exchange and gain full possession of it. We gain a moral right to the property given to us.

Note that there is no other way that we can obtain a moral right to anything. We either get hold of it first or receive it as a gift (or get it in exchange) from someone who has a right to it. On the strong version of the theory we are discussing here there are no other rights. For example, there is no right to inheritance from one's parents. Parents are allowed to bequeath their property to their children, of course, and many do, but they need not do so. Once again, there exists no positive right to aid or assistance for those who are in need of it. Finally, if someone attempts to take property from someone who owns it, the owner has the right to resist this attempt with all the force that is necessary to defend the property. And if, nevertheless, the attempt succeeds, the owner of the property has a right, irrespective of the legal situation, to take it back.

Besides the principles of acquisition and transfer, there is also a principle of rectification. According to the moral rights theory, what morality comes to in the final analysis is simply respect for existing moral rights. A person who lives peacefully, tends to his or her own business and does not violate the rights of anyone else is doing what morality requires of him or her. Even if this person is living high and letting die, that is, even if this person does nothing to help those who, through no fault of their own, happen to be starving to death, there is no room for a moral complaint. This person is living in accordance with the moral law.

No one is allowed to kill anyone else according to the moral rights theory, unless the killing takes place on request (such as in euthanasia), but each person is allowed to kill him- or herself (also with the assistance of another consenting person, as in physician-assisted suicide). And the moral rights theory has nothing to object to in the survival lottery described in the previous chapter, where everyone who takes part in the lottery has

given his or her informed consent. However, according to the
moral rights theory as developed by Nozick (in contradistinction
to Locke's version), there is no obligation to save the lives of
others.

With respect to the trolley examples described in the opening
chapter, the moral rights view sides with ethical egoism and
accepts that we do not flick the switch in the first case. By not
flicking the switch we do not kill the five on track, we merely
allow them to die. But the view accepts that we can flick the
switch if we wish to do so. Then we kill one innocent person, but
this is not intentional killing and hence it is acceptable. In this it
is similar to the sanctity of life doctrine. Moreover, the view is
similar to the sanctity of life doctrine in that it does not endorse
that we push the big man onto the track in the Footbridge case.
If we did, we would actively and intentionally violate his right to
life.

Some radical consequences of the moral rights theory

The point of departure of the moral rights theory, in particular
in Nozick's version of it, is a radical trust in the individual. The
individual is thought to be capable of taking care of him- or
herself if allowed by others in general, and the state in particular,
to do so. The theory allows that a minimal state be established,
which helps people to protect their rights and regain their property if someone steals it from them. It is possible, according to
Nozick, for rational individuals to agree to an arrangement
whereby the police protect the individuals' right to physical
integrity, where courts of law ensure that contracts are upheld,
and so forth. However, there is no room, according to the theory,
for a system where the state uses taxation to oblige individuals
to give up their property, only because a system of education
or health care is needed in society. The modern welfare state, at
least to the extent that it is motivated by a desire to meet urgent
needs (and not to correct past injustices), is considered to be a
sophisticated system of slavery by Nozick.

Does this not reflect a very complacent view of people who are
in need? I suppose that the adherents of the view would argue
that if people are allowed to live their lives as they see fit, we
should expect that, as a matter of course, those who are needy

will be given the kind of assistance they require. It is the authoritarian welfare state that kills our interest in freely helping each other.

It goes without saying that according to the theory of moral rights the state should not act paternalistically with respect to its subjects. It is up to the individual to do what he or she likes, not only with his or her property, but also with him- or herself. It would be a violation of my rights for the state to want to stop me from abusing drugs, from putting my life in jeopardy through strange contracts, working as a prostitute, and so forth.

Here is a radical example of this. I once happened to have lunch with Robert Nozick and put the following example to him. A famous Swedish multi-millionaire, Peter Wallenberg, was known to be suffering from a heart defect. Suppose I approached him and promised that should he ever need a heart transplant, he could have my heart. I would sell it to him immediately for six million dollars. Suppose Wallenberg had accepted my offer and paid me the price I asked for, would he then have become the moral owner of my heart? Suppose that, a few months later, he needed it? Could he then have taken it from me?

Nozick had no problems with my example. It was obvious, he thought, that it followed from his theory of moral rights, as stated in *Anarchy, State, and Utopia*, that Wallenberg would become the moral owner of my heart. Nozick himself was no longer quite sure that his theory was right, however. But many people still think it is, and it does present an interesting example, so I will continue to focus on the theory in its most radical form, irrespective of what the author of *Anarchy, State, and Utopia* may later have come to think about it.

Are these and other radical consequences of the theory something that should make us reject the theory? Nozick himself may have problems with some examples, but they do not worry adherents of the theory. Why object, for example, to the selling and buying of organs? they ask. When people sell their organs, they probably know what they are doing and they probably have a very good reason to do so. The example I presented to Nozick is not very realistic. In fact, I would not sell my heart on conditions such as the one I mentioned. But many people in poor parts of the world do sell their kidneys. Should they be prevented from doing so? Why? Is a trade in organs immoral? In that case, who is acting immorally? Are those who sell their organs acting immorally? If they are not allowed to sell their organs, they might starve to death or be unable to provide clothing, housing and education for their children. Are those who want to buy the organs committing a moral mistake? Why? Should they suffer instead from renal failure or utilise expensive renal dialysis equipment, needed more urgently by others? Or does a state that tolerates this kind of trade act immorally? In that case, why?

We have seen that the theory of moral rights has no problems with voluntary euthanasia or suicide. According to the moral rights theory, it is up to individuals to give up their lives and to contract someone to kill them, irrespective of the quality of their future lives or the consequences for other people of their death. In this the theory of moral rights is even more liberal than utilitarianism (in fact, it is even more liberal than ethical egoism). For similar reasons the theory can accept the survival lottery described in the previous chapter. In all this it differs from the sanctity of life doctrine. But the theory does not, in general, allow us to kill one person who has not consented to this in order to save the lives of three. In this it is similar to the sanctity of life doctrine.

Consider the following example. Anna has devoted her life to Amnesty International. She is divorced. She has four children who have lived most of the time with their father. It has not been possible for her to take them with her on her missions to a South America ruled by dictators. She is now travelling in Argentina with her four children, however, only a few months after the establishment of a democratic regime there. She is terminally ill and realises that she has only a short time left to live. She wants to show her children something of the kind of life she has led. Her lecture tour has come to an end. She spends the last night in Buenos Aires. Amnesty has provided her and her children with accommodation. They are staying with one of the local members of the organisation. After her children have gone to bed she takes a nightcap with her host, Pedro. Pedro now takes her by surprise. He has conned the local Amnesty group, he confesses. He is a former torturer and he has invited Anna to stay with him for a very special reason. He has had more than enough of her human rights talk, he says. He has gathered some of his former friends and he is now going to teach Anna a lesson: the end justifies the means. His friends enter the room, carrying automatic weapons. He offers a syringe to Anna. It contains a fatal dose of potassium chloride, he tells her. He now wants her to kill her eldest son, Peter, who is asleep in the next room, suffering from a slight temperature. Pedro threatens that unless Anna kills her son, he will make sure that all her children are killed instantly.

Anna realises that the threat is genuine. To her own surprise, she finds herself grabbing the syringe and walking into the nearby room. Her son wakes up, complains that he feels dizzy and asks what is going on. Anna tells him that she is going to give him an injection. Then his fever will go away, she says. She injects the poison and her son dies. Pedro is satisfied.

The next day Anna tells her three remaining children that their brother is dead. His fever turned out to be more serious than anyone had expected, she says. There is no time for ceremonies. The local Amnesty group will organise the funeral. Now they have to hurry. They immediately embark on the ferry to Montevideo. Anna returns the children to their father, who is waiting for them, and tells him that the fever killed their eldest son. He accepts her explanation. She then goes to a hospice where she is to spend her last few months.

Several years have passed since this happened. Anna is dead. The three brothers and sisters lead good and protected lives together with their father. They rarely speak of their deceased brother, but they sometimes think of him. The thought causes some pain, but they all know perfectly well how to get on with their own lives. And they remember their mother with pride. She worked for a noble cause, they say. They know nothing of Anna's action. What are we to say of it?

From a utilitarian point of view, and from the point of view of ethical egoism of the contractual variety, there is much to be said in defence of Anna's action. It is certainly true that if Anna was found out, even a utilitarian or egoist may claim that there should be some kind of punishment for what she has done. However, she was never found out ('Anna' was not her real name). Moreover, considering the very special circumstances, the punishment would have to be lenient anyway. It may be difficult then to understand how Anna could act as she did. Was she not bound by such strong inhibitions that it was impossible for her to kill her child? Perhaps she did have strong inhibitions of this kind, but the situation was exceptional and so was she. She knew a great deal about the realities of life under military dictatorships. It was not difficult for her to take the threat seriously. And she knew that she herself was dying. She may have felt that it would have been selfish of her not to save at least three of her children when it was in her power to do so.

From the point of view of deontological ethics, and from the point of view of the sanctity of life doctrine in particular, what Anna did was murder. She should rather have allowed all of her children to be killed than kill one of them herself.

We see that in this judgement the moral rights theory concurs. By killing her eldest son, who did not consent to this, Anna violated his right to life. Her action was wrong and it was seriously wrong. The end does not justify the means.

Capital punishment

According to the moral rights theory, what punishment would be appropriate for Anna if it had been possible to punish her? Kant would not have hesitated: Anna deserved to be executed. But what is an adherent of the moral rights theory to say of her? The adherents of the moral rights theory look just as seriously upon what Anna has done. But what kind of punishment would be appropriate for her according to the moral rights theory? What kind of theory of punishment in general is dictated by the moral rights theory?

While the deontological theory focuses exclusively on the criminal, in order to give him the punishment he deserves, the moral rights theory focuses exclusively on the victim. This aspect of the theory of moral rights is rarely discussed, and many of its adherents, such as Locke and Nozick, tend to combine it with a deontological theory of retributive justice. However, the theory of moral rights should also be taken seriously as a theory about crime and punishment. If taken seriously and if stripped of all retributivist ideas, it would say something like the following.

The victim has a right to what he or she has been deprived of, or else is due fair compensation. And that compensation should include not only what has been removed, but also the costs of regaining it. This is easy to understand when applied to crimes such as theft and trespass, but what are the adherents of the moral rights theory to say of murder? Is it possible for murderers to compensate their victims?

This is in one obvious sense impossible. And this means that if we want to abide by a strict version of the moral rights theory, we must accept that there is no room for the punishment of murder. There is no denying that when we want to guard ourselves against murder, we may resort to all kinds of means according to the theory. In order to protect my life, I may kill the person who attacks me. However, if I fail and he kills me, then there is no further room for any just action against the murderer.

Could we not say that our murderer should pay compensation to our relatives? No, this argument sits ill with the moral rights theory. Our relatives do not possess us. The murderer has not deprived them of any property of theirs. The only way someone can come to have a just complaint to make about my murder would be if I had previously sold some part of me to someone else. If I have sold my heart to Peter Wallenberg, as in the example above, then Peter Wallenberg can demand just compensation from my murderer, of course. No one else is in a position to do so.

We noted that deontological retributivism is not interested in crime prevention. The punishment is there for the sake of the perpetrator, not for the sake of society. If the punishment has a preventive effect, then this is a second, and not sought-for, effect. This explains why sometimes retributivists want *less* harsh punishments than utilitarians. In a similar vein, the theory of moral rights, if taken seriously, is not interested primarily in crime prevention through punishment. According to the moral rights view, the state ought not to use the criminal as a means to deterrence from future crime. In this it is similar to deontological ethics. Yet in another respect it is very different from the deontological view. While the theory of moral rights makes plenty of room for the police, for locks and security vaults, for violent resistance whenever someone tries to thwart the rights of someone else, and if necessary for restitution, it makes no room whatever for what we can genuinely call 'punishment'.

If this analysis is correct, then the theory of moral rights must reject, for principled reasons, capital punishment. For even if we want very much to do so, there is no way for us to compensate a victim of murder.

Can the moral rights theory be applied?

A problem with utilitarianism, we might recall, is that it is difficult to apply the theory. If it can be applied at all, it can only be applied indirectly. The theory prescribes a method of decision-making which is possible to abide by in the hope that, if consistently applied, in the long run, the method will have at least as good consequences as any alternative decision method we can think of. The theory of moral rights faces a similar problem. The theory contains three tenets: first of all, a principle of acquisitions; second, a principle of transfer; and third, a principle of rectification. The third principle is operative as soon as the first two principles have been violated. But how are we to rectify injustices committed in the past? Who owns a certain piece of land in the USA? In order to answer this question we must conduct counterfactual speculation of the following kind. Who would have possessed this land today if the USA had not been colonised as it was, which is clearly at variance with the moral rights theory? It is doubtful whether any exact answer to a question like this exists, and it is obvious that there is no way for us to find out.

Cannot the adherent of the theory of moral rights have recourse to a decision procedure that allows him or her at least to approximate justice? Would it not be reasonable to assume, for example, that those who are worst off in today's society are the descendants of those who, historically speaking, have been wronged the most? So why not try to expunge the results of past injustices once and for all by making sure that those who are worst off get compensation? Would not the best method, as a rough rule of thumb, be to have a radical redistribution (if not full-blown socialism) to the advantage of those who are worst off in the short term? We could arrange this, as Nozick puts it, as a 'punishment for old sins'.

This is not convincing. First of all, it is doubtful whether any solid empirical foundation exists for this very speculative argument. Second, and even more importantly, it is doubtful whether it helps much if such a foundation does exist. For the moral rights theory is a theory of absolute side-constraints to our actions. In this it is similar to deontological ethics. So it is hard to believe that such a theory can endorse a rule of thumb intended to *approximate* justice. According to the theory, the important thing is that we never violate any rights and that if rights have been violated, the wrongs created are rectified. It is not a theory asking us to approximate justice by maximising the number of just actions or minimising the number of injustices.

Note, however, that even if it is true that there is no easy way to apply the theory of moral rights, this does not mean that the theory must be mistaken. The adherent of the theory can respond, as did some utilitarians, with the following question: Who said that true morality must be easily applicable?

Should we accept the moral rights theory?

The moral rights theory may attract those who find the argument against utilitarianism, that it imposes too heavy demands, a plausible one. Just like egoism, the moral rights theory allows you to live high and let die – at least to the extent that those who die do not do so because you have actively wronged them. In one respect the moral rights theory is even more relaxed than egoism. While egoism makes it part and parcel of your moral duty to care for your own best interests, the moral rights theory just allows you to do so. At the same time, the theory does avoid the objection raised against utilitarianism that it gives the moral agent too much licence. According to the moral rights theory, it is not right to kill one person in order to save the lives of others. However, all this does not mean that there are no problems connected with the theory of moral rights. Those who do not find that, according to utilitarianism, we have too strict moral duties will find it strange that we have no moral reason to help those who are in need. I suspect that, in particular, people who *are* in need will find this strange. Some will also find that the theory is too liberal in its dealing with suicide and euthanasia. Is it really true, they will ask, that I have a right to kill myself, even if this results in severe problems for those who are near and dear to me?

And is it true that the consequences for people in general, if we practise a system of euthanasia, are of no importance? It is one thing to argue that a system of euthanasia does not give rise to a slippery slope leading to a society in which everybody must come to fear for his or her life and hesitate to seek medical attention. This is what many utilitarians, defending such a system, have argued. But can it also be true that such a slippery slope argument is morally *irrelevant*? This is what the adherent of the moral rights theory must claim.

Like utilitarianism, the moral rights theory can accept a survival lottery. It does not accept, however, the killing of one person (who does not consent) in order to save three lives. It is questionable whether the moral rights theory or utilitarianism gives the right answer here. The reader should think carefully about this question. Did Anna do the right thing, or should she have allowed all her children to be killed? In the trolley example, is it all right or simply wrong to push the big man onto the track? In the final chapter we will return to this question.

The moral rights theory has a special problem with abortion and the moral status of animals. Some advocates of a moral rights theory have wanted to take part in the movement defending the rights of animals. This is true in particular of the American philosopher Tom Regan. When defining what it means to be a 'moral subject', these thinkers have defended very inclusive criteria, allowing that many animals (all mammals) are moral subjects. However, it then transpires that even foetuses are moral subjects. So these thinkers must concur in the deontological rejection of abortion as being just as bad as murder. Others have wanted to defend abortion, making rather strict requirements when defining what it means to be a 'moral subject'. These thinkers, most notably the American philosopher Michael Tooley, have come to defend not only abortion and the killing of animals, but infanticide as well.

It seems that here we face a troublesome theoretical difficulty with the moral rights theory, a difficulty it shares with deontological ethics. Both approaches employ a notion of moral status, allowing that some entities have, and others lack, moral status. This notion is conceived of in absolute terms: either you are, or you are not, an *innocent human being* (deontological ethics) or a *moral subject* (the theory of moral rights). This means that the adherents of these respective theories become embroiled in difficult metaphysical speculation. When does human life begin? When do we become moral subjects (persons)?

The adherents of utilitarianism and egoism of the contractual variety need not enter into these speculations. They can adopt a pragmatic stance to the problem of abortion and infanticide, allowing infanticide in primitive societies lacking access to methods of contraception and safe abortion, while prohibiting infanticide in modern societies with contraception and free access to safe abortion.

With respect to animals their ways part, however. The utilitarian must take the welfare of sentient animals as seriously as the welfare of human beings. To the egoist, however, the suffering of animals is of no direct moral concern. Animals cannot take part in any social contract. As we have seen, some moral rights theorists side with utilitarianism on this point, while others side with egoism.

Further reading about moral rights

John Locke's *Two Treatises of Government* (1689) exists in many editions. The quotation from J. S. Mill is from 'Utilitarianism', in Mary Warnock (ed.), *Utilitarianism* (London: Collins/Fontana, 1962). Jeremy Bentham discusses the French declaration of rights in 'A Critical Examination of the Declaration of Rights', in Bhikhu Parekh (ed.), *Bentham's Political Thought* (London: Croom Helm, 1973). For an instructive treatment of the subject of utilitarianism and rights, see L. W. Sumner, *The Moral Foundation of Rights* (Oxford: Clarendon Press, 1987). Robert Nozick states his theory of moral rights in *Anarchy, State, and Utopia* (Oxford: Blackwell, 1974). He modified his position later, but he never returned to it in any systematic fashion. Other contemporary defences of moral rights can be found in M. N. Rothbard, *The Ethics of Liberty* (Atlantic Highlands, NJ: Humanities Press, 1982) and Jan Narveson, *The Libertarian Idea* (Philadelphia: Temple University Press, 1988). For (politically) radical critiques of Nozick's interpretation of Locke's proviso, see G. A. Cohen, *Self-Ownership, Freedom, and Equality* (Cambridge: Cambridge University Press, 1995) and Hillel Steiner, *An Essay on Rights* (Oxford: Blackwell, 1994). Tom Regan's defence of animal rights is put forward in *The Case for Animal Rights* (Berkeley: University of California Press, 1983). Regan is attacked by R. G. Frey in *Rights, Killing and Suffering: Moral Vegetarianism and Applied Ethics* (Oxford: Blackwell, 1983). For detailed arguments for and against Nozick's position, see David Schmidtz (ed.), *Robert Nozick* (New York: Cambridge University Press, 2002).

6

Virtue Ethics

Introduction

So far we have discussed four different ideas about what makes right actions right and wrong actions wrong: utilitarianism, ethical egoism, Kantianism and theories of fundamental moral rights. I now turn to a very different moral approach: virtue ethics. According to the adherents of virtue ethics, the reason that it is difficult to make a choice among the different moral theories discussed so far may be that we are focusing on the wrong question. Instead of asking what it is that makes a right action right we ought to focus on the question: what kind of person ought I to be? The answer to this question is not a criterion of right action in general, but some kind of list of virtues.

Virtue ethics is a moral approach taken up most famously by Aristotle. As a matter of fact, most philosophers during antiquity expressed their moral philosophy in the form of virtue ethics of one kind or another. The recent interest in virtue ethics originates, however, with an article by the British moral philosopher Elizabeth Anscombe, 'Modern Moral Philosophy', published in 1958. Ever since, the philosophical world has witnessed a growing interest in the subject.

A point of departure for this book is the idea that a fundamental problem of ethics is what we ought to do in particular situations. Ethics should help us solve such practical problems. So the claim that we ought to focus on the virtues instead of focusing on normative questions will not be taken at face value. My intention is to bring virtue ethics, if possible, into competition with the other views discussed in this book. I do not deny that it may be a good idea to focus on the virtues rather than on normative problems. As a matter of fact, all moral views discussed thus far have answers to the question what sort of person I should try to be. Their lists of virtues, however, are derived from their criterion of right action. When we discuss virtue ethics we want to know how *its* list of the virtues connects to the normative question. Unless we understand this, we will not understand to what extent virtue ethics presents us with an *alternative* to utilitarianism, egoism, Kantianism and moral rights theories, or is merely a complement to these theories. So in what follows I shall discuss how virtue ethics, in different forms, relates to normative theories like the ones just discussed.

The virtues

Typical of virtue ethics is its interest in general traits of character – in contradistinction to traits of personality. It is assumed then, or stipulated, that traits of character can somehow be developed through training or education while traits of personality are more or less fixed through our biology. Virtue ethicists define certain character traits or dispositions and think of them as desirable. In effect, all virtue theorists provide us with *lists* of those traits of character that *are* virtues. Typical items on these lists are such things as courage, temperance, wisdom and justice (the 'cardinal' moral virtues), but also generosity, benevolence, constancy and industry. There is no unanimity among virtue ethicists about the items that belong to the list or about how in detail each item is to be understood.

What are we to make of these conflicts among virtue ethicists? Does their disagreement show that there are no *true* virtues to put on the list, or that the virtues are *relative to time and place*? Most famously, Alasdair MacIntyre has argued that disagreement indicates relativism, but his line of argument is not irresistible. For all the conflicting ideas among virtue ethicists, there may well exist a definite list of the *true* virtues (perhaps yet to be found). And, as we shall see, most virtue ethicists provide an answer to the question: what makes a trait of character a virtue? They provide a criterion that can be used to decide whether a certain trait of character belongs to the list of the virtues.

However, many virtue ethicists are silent on the following normative questions. Why ought I to be virtuous? How do the virtues connect to normative questions in general? It is a striking fact about much of the new literature in this field that no clear answer to questions of this kind is provided. This is true of important, much discussed and anthologised contributions such as Philippa Foot's 'Virtues and Vices' and Iris Murdoch's *The Sovereignty of Good*. But there are exceptions to this rule. Here I will concentrate on such exceptions, that is, I will concentrate on defences of virtue ethics that do provide an answer to this question, and, in order to cover the entire field, I will also speculate about such answers which are merely possible.

Virtue ethics and normative ethics

Three main possibilities seem to be open for the virtue ethicist who is prepared to say something explicitly about the relation between the virtues and normative problems (of right and wrong action).

First of all, virtue ethics may be considered to provide a criterion of right action. So, if we develop these virtues and act on them, we will as a matter of fact act rightly. And our actions will be right *because* we who perform them are virtuous agents, or perhaps because these actions are such that they *would be* performed by a virtuous agent.

Second, virtue ethics may be considered to provide us with an answer to what kinds of characteristics we ought to develop in ourselves and to foster in our children, but to no other normative questions. So, by developing these virtues we do only what we ought to do, and no more.

Third, virtue ethics may be considered to provide us with a plausible method of moral decision-making, which either helps us to solve hard practical problems or helps us at least to steer clear of some kinds of immoral behaviour that we are otherwise prone to. All this means that if we develop these virtues, we become *more likely* to act rightly.

Let me now consider these three possibilities in order.

Do the virtues provide us with a plausible criterion of right action?

Not infrequently virtue ethics is described in a manner that invites the interpretation that it provides us with a statement of a criterion of rightness. Consider, for example, the following statement of one central tenet of virtue ethics by one influential recent representative of the tradition, Rosalind Hursthouse:

> An action is right iff [if and only if] it is what a virtuous agent would do in the circumstances. ('Virtue Theory and Abortion', p. 218)

This suggests that the author conceives of virtue ethics as providing us with a statement of a criterion of rightness of actions. This is not the only possible interpretation, however. Does Hursthouse really mean not only that the actions that a virtuous person would perform are right, but also that they are right because a virtuous person would perform them? Let us just assume that this is how the 'if and only if' clause is to be interpreted. Then we face an example of a virtue ethics providing us with a criterion of right action, in competition with utilitarianism, egoism, Kantianism and theories of moral rights.

Virtue ethics conceived of as an ethical theory providing a criterion of rightness has sometimes been rejected too hastily. It has been argued that since a good character is a character that tends to lead to right actions, the rightness of the actions it leads to cannot be explained in terms of it. This would lead us into a vicious circle. But the virtue ethicist need not argue that a good character is good because it tends to lead to right actions. The good character can be characterised in empirical terms. Some recent virtue ethicists accept Aristotle's view that the content of a virtuous character is determined by our human nature. A virtuous person is a flourishing human being. Others argue with the American philosopher Michael Slote that there is a plurality of traits which we commonly find admirable in human beings in certain circumstances; these traits are characteristic of virtue.

So virtue ethics need not be circular. But does it provide us with a plausible criterion of rightness? Does it strike us as a worthy candidate in the competition with which we are now familiar? Is it preferable to utilitarianism, egoism, deontological ethics or the ethics of rights?

Several problems face the adherent of virtue ethics so conceived. First of all, *being such that a virtuous person would perform it* can hardly be a right-making characteristic of an action. We cannot explain the putative (moral) fact that a certain action should be performed with reference to the fact that it would be performed by a virtuous person, even if this person were a flourishing human being or such that we tend to admire him or her. The explanation of why the action is right (if it is) must minimally refer to some concrete aspect of the situation where the action is performed. It must refer to the *actual* motive of the person who performed it, to some *internal* aspect of the action itself or to the *consequences* for those who are affected by it. Did it harm anyone? Did it violate any rights? Or so it seems to me.

But if it is true that a virtuous person would perform the action, must not this be the case because the action has certain concrete characteristics by virtue of which it would be selected? And do not these characteristics explain its rightness? This may very well be the case. However, in that case, these characteristics *themselves*, not the fact that the action would be chosen by a virtuous agent, make the action right. So the virtue of the agent does not enter into the moral explanation of the rightness of the action after all.

Virtue ethics could, of course, be conceived of as the idea that 'right' *means* 'would be performed by a virtuous person' or that rightness is somehow *constituted* in terms of virtue. However, these are *metaethical* views, saying something about the meaning or function of 'right', and thus are not in competition with the *normative* views discussed in this book. Even if we were to concede that 'right' means 'would be performed by a virtuous agent', we would still want to know which actions possess this characteristic; utilitarianism, egoism, deontology and the theory of moral rights may be conceived of as putative answers to this question.

But could we not then make the normative claim that an action is right if and only if it is *actually* performed by a virtuous person, and otherwise wrong? Slote has characterised this position as 'agent-based' virtue ethics. This may seem more promising. Let us say that an action is right if and only if it is performed by a virtuous person and otherwise wrong. And if it is right, it is right *because* a virtuous person performs it, and if it is wrong, it is wrong *because* a vicious person performs it. There are problems even with this suggestion, however.

In the first place, this *exclusive* focus on the agent may seem strange. Must not the reason that the action is right or wrong have *something* to do with what happens to those who are affected by it? This is a question that will be raised at least by utilitarians, egoists and moral rights theorists alike.

Second, is it not strange if only virtuous persons can perform right actions – be they flourishing human beings or admirable persons? After all, should not morality provide instruction even for those of us who are seriously wanting in terms of virtue? But if having a virtuous character is a right-making characteristic, and lack of virtue, or the presence of vice, a wrong-making characteristic, then there is no way that a vicious person can ever act rightly.

Finally, this version of virtue ethics has the strange implication that whatever action a virtuous person might perform (even a horrendous action) would be right.

In order to meet this last objection, Slote has developed a subtle version of the theory. In order for an action to be right, according to this version, it is necessary but not sufficient that a virtuous agent performs it. And in order for an action to be wrong, it is necessary but not sufficient that a vicious person performs it. In both cases, something more is required:

> Acts ... do not count as admirable or virtuous for an agent-based theory ... merely because they are or would be done by someone who in fact is admirable or possesses admirable motivation – they have to exhibit, express, or further such motivation or be such that they *would* exhibit, etc., such motivation if they occurred, in order to qualify as admirable or virtuous. ('Agent-Based Virtue Ethics', p. 244)

A way of understanding this would be as follows. An act is right if and only if it *reflects* (which is here shorthand for 'exhibits, expresses or furthers') good motivation, and it is wrong if and only if it *reflects* bad motivation. This means that Slote has strengthened both the criterion of right action and the criterion of wrong action. Not only must an action, in order to be right, be performed by a virtuous agent; it must *reflect* the virtuous character of the person who performs it as well. And not only must an action, in order to be wrong, be performed by a vicious person, it must also *reflect* the vicious character of the person who performs it.

It may seem that if we strengthen both the criterion of right action and the criterion of wrong action, then this must leave many cases undecided. We will have a class of actions lacking normative status; they are neither right nor wrong. This may seem counterintuitive, and it is certainly at variance with the claim that morality should guide our actions. However, to the extent that only *hypothetical* actions lack normative status, this defect may seem to be of little importance. Horrendous actions performed by a virtuous person are in this sense merely hypothetical. As a matter of fact, a virtuous person never performs horrendous actions. However, the case is different and more troublesome with a vicious person. It is easy to imagine situations where a vicious person performs a generous action. When he or she does, the action does not reflect the agent's character, of course. We have to explain it differently. We have to say, for example, that the reason that this truly vicious person performs a certain generous action must be that he or she wants to promote his or her career, or fears being exposed and subjected to punishment, and so forth. Such actions are very common indeed. And it is counterintuitive (and even moralistic) to claim that they lack normative status. These actions are, in my opinion at any rate, right actions. Moreover, there are numerous cases where a virtuous person performs actions that do not reflect his or her virtuous character (like getting out of bed in the morning).

A way of avoiding the problem with actions lacking normative status would be to introduce new normative categories. It seems as though we would need at least four different categories. (1) There are actions that are *perfectly right*, that is, actions performed by a virtuous person and reflecting their agent's virtuous character. (2) There are actions that are in a new category, let us call them *right*, that is, actions performed by a virtuous person but not reflecting the virtuous character of their agent. (3) There are actions that are also in a new category, let us call them *all right*, that is, actions performed by a vicious person but not reflecting the vicious character of their agent. (4) There are actions that are *wrong,* that is, actions performed by a vicious person and reflecting the agent's vicious character.

However, it may seem that this does not only mean normative complication but normative confusion as well. Suppose I have two options: either I become a monk, develop a virtuous character and perform only perfectly right or right actions – but, alas, make little difference to the world as such. Or I become a vicious person who, as a matter of fact, by mostly acting out of character and performing actions that are all right, make an enormous difference (for the better) to the world. Which option is it 'preferable' (to use a neutral term) for me to adopt? The question boggles the mind.

Note that, as we saw in Chapter 4, Kant faced a similar problem when defending both his categorical imperative and the idea
that we ought to act from the right motive (a good will).

Ought we to choose the virtues for their own sake?

We have found reasons to doubt that the virtues figure in an
essential way in any plausible criterion of right action. But
perhaps we have misconceived our problem altogether. We have
tried to see whether virtue ethics provides a criterion of right
action in competition with more traditional criteria such as the
ones given by utilitarianism, egoism, Kantianism and theories
of moral rights, and we have found virtue ethics wanting. But
perhaps the problem with the traditional approaches to ethics is
not that, in the final analysis, they give the wrong answers to the
right question, but rather that they start from a false assumption:
the very question they set out to answer is the wrong one. We
should not be so obsessed with normative questions. We should
stop thinking about what to do in abstract thought-examples like
the trolley one. Instead, we should focus on the virtues and try to
find out which they are. What traits of character are valuable?

A statement of this position can be found in the article by
Anscombe mentioned earlier that inaugurated the new interest in
virtue ethics:

> [T]he concepts of obligation, and duty – *moral* obligation and *moral*
> duty, that is to say – and of what is *morally* right and wrong, and of
> the *moral* sense of 'ought', ought to be jettisoned if this is psycho-
> logically possible ... It would be a great improvement if, instead of
> 'morally wrong', one always named a genus such as 'untruthful',
> 'unchaste', 'unjust'. ('Modern Moral Philosophy', pp. 26, 34)

But could a search for the virtues go on completely unperturbed
by *any* normative considerations whatever? I think not. If it does,
the result will be of little moral importance. However, the normative question we ought to focus on is perhaps not what makes
right actions right (in general) but, more narrowly, on what traits
of characters we ought to foster in ourselves (and in our children
through education). Virtue ethics may provide an answer to this
more narrow class of normative questions, setting the rest of
them to one side. Perhaps virtue ethics provides us with a
criterion of rightness *applicable only to decisions relevant to*

moral development and education. This is the move to be discussed in the present section.

There are two problems with this move in defence of virtue ethics. One is that it relegates the virtues to a very marginal role in ethics. The other, more important one is that it leads to inconsistency or ad hoc solutions.

Take first the problem of marginality. It is strange if an ethical theory should only address the problem of rightness of actions in relation to a narrowly circumscribed class of actions (our choice of traits of character in our moral development and education). After all, our moral life consists of so much more than this. It is hard to believe that an adequate morality could be silent about this.

Moreover, if we hold that virtue ethics does provide us with a criterion of rightness, but a criterion only of rightness of some actions (to do with moral development and education), we run the risk that compliance with this criterion may mean that we act wrongly on some other, quite general criterion of rightness, such as the ones suggested by utilitarianism, egoism, deontological ethics or the theory of moral rights. This would happen if we were to develop a certain virtue in a situation where this would lead to bad consequences – or come to flout the demands of the categorical imperative or violate any rights. In order to counter this possibility, the virtue ethicist, who has narrowed his or her moral theory to state a criterion of rightness of actions to do with moral development and education only, would have to claim that all these competing claims are false. However, this move would leave the rest of morality covered by no criterion of rightness at all, which would not only be strange but a very sad fact indeed. Or the virtue ethicist may hold that while utilitarianism, or egoism, or Kantianism, or the theory of moral rights, or some other moral theory may be true in general, this otherwise true moral theory must be silent about problems to do with moral development and education. But this is utterly ad hoc. If what makes right actions right is that they maximise welfare, or conform to the categorical imperative, or violate no moral rights, or whatever we may think of, why should not this be true also of our decisions related to moral development and education? Remember that egoism (contractualism), utilitarianism and Kantianism each recommends certain desirable traits of character as well.

Virtue ethics and moral expertise

If we develop the virtues, does this mean that we become better moral agents? One idea could be this. By developing the virtues, or at least some of them, we become moral experts. Now we realise better what we ought to do. We are capable of solving hard practical problems. Another idea would be this. By developing the virtues we become persons who do the right thing by habit or spontaneously. In this section I discuss the former idea. In the next section I will discuss the latter idea.

There is much to be said in defence of either of them. How do we solve hard practical problems? We saw in the introductory chapter that we need to have recourse to plausible moral principles as well as a grasp of the relevant facts. Can there be experts on this? Can a kind of virtue be described that is characteristic of a person who is good at solving hard practical problems?

The virtue we should look at now is obviously the virtue of practical wisdom or, as Aristotle called it, *phronesis*. Is there such a thing as practical wisdom? How should we characterise it? How can we acquire it?

Can there be expertise in finding out which are the true moral principles, if there are any, or, at any rate, what kind of principles are of importance in a certain particular case? I suppose there can be such expertise. A typical expert on this would obviously be a talented moral philosopher (normative ethicist).

Note that we cannot tell the talented from the less talented moral philosopher from the conclusion of his or her argument. People who are obviously very talented moral philosophers disagree about the right answer to the question about the correct moral point of departure for the solution of practical questions. However, I do believe that those philosophers who are talented have something in common, irrespective of what moral conclusion they end up with. They are imaginative, they are capable of conducting counterfactual arguments, they have a feeling for the fact that even if some consequences of a certain principle may seem counterintuitive, this may not be the last word about the principle in question. Other principles face other difficulties and, in the final analysis, it is important to try to find the best explanation of those moral intuitions that we are prepared to retain after careful examination. (More about this in the final chapter.)

A problem with the characteristic is that it is rather inclusive. It seems possible to be a good moral philosopher even if one is not a good human being. I will return to this point below. Moreover, it is of little avail merely to be good at normative ethics (abstractly speaking) when a practical problem is to be solved. For the fact that competent moral philosophers reach conflicting results when applying normative ethics to abstract cases indicates that the way of solving hard practical questions cannot be first of all to find out what the true moral principles are and then apply them. In that case the solution to all practical problems might have to wait for another 2,000 years or so.

So perhaps it is more important that an expert on solving hard practical problems is well versed in *alternative* normative outlooks and capable of finding spots where many different basic moral outlooks point in the same direction, where it is possible to find what John Rawls has famously called an overlapping consensus. Moreover, this person must be good at identifying facts in the situation that are indeed relevant to the various different basic moral outlooks. A knack for probability calculus is probably useful as well for a moral expert.

But not only intellectual capacities are of importance. A moral expert must also have certain emotive capacities. A capacity to identify with other creatures is of crucial importance. But what is equally needed is a capacity for impartiality. In order to be impartial, I submit, moral experts must know a good deal about themselves. Why do they feel the way they do, why do they have the preferences they have? Unless their characters survive scrutiny of this kind it is very likely that, without acknowledging this themselves, they will be biased in their judgements.

We could go on for a long while discussing these and other putative characteristics of a wise person, that is, a person who is good at solving hard practical questions. But there is no denying that something along the lines just adumbrated must be part of the notion. However, note that the characterisation is still very inclusive. It seems as though even a thoroughly nasty person could be able to exhibit these characteristics. And it is certainly true that, in some professional settings, people that we would not like to invite for dinner have done a very good job. The late US president Richard Nixon (also known as Tricky Dicky) showed great skill in foreign affairs and eventually found a way to bring an end to the terrible war in Vietnam, we should remember.

Nobler figures who had held the office before him had been unable to do so.

Is this where an analogy put forward by Aristotle between phronesis and perception is in place? Is it possible for the virtuous person simply to 'perceive' what ought to be done? No. If it is true that what we ought to do may relate in some way to the actual consequences of our actions, as compared to the consequences of various different possible alternative actions, it is not open to inspection. In order to answer the question of what we should do, we must make inferences. And all sorts of very complex information may be relevant to these inferences. So, all kinds of talents and skills, which can be exhibited by virtuous and vicious persons alike, are needed here.

Virtue as a guard against immoral action

Are the virtues of any assistance when we want to avoid certain kinds of nasty behaviour, to which as human beings we sometimes seem prone? If we develop the virtues, does this mean that we will not so easily become victims of all sorts of temptation? This is an aspect of the virtues that has been stressed, for example, by Philippa Foot, known not only for her trolley example but also for her defence of virtue ethics:

> I shall now turn to another thesis about the virtues, which I might express by saying that they are *corrective*, each one standing at a point at which there is some temptation to be resisted or deficiency of motivation to be made good. As Aristotle put it, virtues are about what is difficult for men. ('Virtues and Vices', p. 169)

Now, in many situations we can do with less than virtue if we want to avoid yielding to temptation. In most professional settings, for example, we simply want people to reach morally reasonable answers to the question of what should be done, and to act on these answers as well. This presupposes, for example, that health care personnel are prepared to do their job, but not that they have *in general* very good characters. Doing their job includes treating their patients as individual persons with individual interests, and tending to these interests in a professional fashion. Even an evil person can do this. The same could be said about other professions. If we like, here we may speak of 'professional' virtues. But then, of course, we must acknowledge the importance of such virtues.

However, the role of professional virtues is derivative and not fundamental. Their content must be determined by a critical examination of the corresponding institution (profession). If there is something morally wrong about the design of the institution (profession) or its goal, it might be a good thing not to be prepared to act professionally. In our relations with those who are near and dear to us there may seem to be more room for the virtues properly conceived of as (very general) traits of character. If I am a virtuous person, then I am kind (habitually) to my children – I treat them well spontaneously, or out of habit.

This is all right when it comes to those who are near and dear. If I am a nurse, I should not treat my patients well out of kindness, however. I should not treat them the way I do because of any personal relations I may have developed with them. On the contrary, I ought to care for them *irrespective* of my personal feelings for them. I ought to be impartial and professional with respect to them. But the situation with those who are near and dear *is* different. So it may seem that there is some room for the virtues here.

However, in close relationships it seems as though even people who are in general very odious may be able to behave decently. Even Adolf Hitler seems to have treated his mistress Eva Braun in a loving, caring and respectful manner. This may be a disturbing psychological fact, but it is still a fact. So perhaps we should speak here of certain familial virtues rather than of virtues in general. And even these familial virtues should be held to scrutiny. Our interest in the well-being of those who are near and dear to us may go too far; this interest may, if taken to extremes, mean that we pay insufficient attention to the suffering or moral rights of strangers.

But would it not at least be somewhat helpful, in both professional and personal settings, if people were *generally* more virtuous? Would it not mean that they had received a kind of 'vaccination' against certain kinds of horrible action? Even if tempted to do so, a virtuous person would not take advantage of the weakness of other persons that are dependent on him or her. A virtuous person would not only function well in certain well-known professional or private settings, he or she would also resist temptation in new and unprecedented circumstances. A truly virtuous person would be able also to sustain the institutions of a good society. This seems to be the idea put forward above, with reference to Aristotle, by Philippa Foot.

All this would be fine if it were possible. However, there are critics of virtue ethics that insist that this general kind of virtue is always fragile. Experimental data indicate that we may come to lose our virtue when our need for it is most pressing (under temptation). If the 'situationist' experimental tradition in social and personality psychology is on the right track, then it seems as though behavioural variation across a population owes more to situational differences than to dispositional differences among persons. There are no robust traits of character.

If this is true, which is of course controversial, then, in our attempts to avoid patients and students being treated badly, we should invest more hope in public surveillance and in virtues specific to the professions than in the possibility of instilling through education or training general (robust) traits of character. And if we want a more humane society, we should focus more on the institutions of this society and less on the very general traits of character of its citizens. This seems, by the way, to be the moral to be drawn from the German author Bertholt Brecht's admirably subtle play *The Good Person of Sichuan*.

Conclusion

If my argument in this chapter is sound, then we have found reasons to doubt that virtue ethics can provide us with any plausible criterion of right action in competition with utilitarianism, egoism, deontological ethics or the theory of moral rights. But the virtues are of importance, and it might be a good idea to focus more exclusively on them; to try to find out what characterises a moral expert (a wise person) who is capable of solving hard and pressing practical questions. We may want to listen to such experts, if we can identify them, before we make up our own minds about what to do. And it might be a good idea to try to develop, and to teach our children, traits of habit that can to some degree 'vaccinate' them against all sorts of nasty behaviour that were typical of the century we have recently left behind. We want to teach them not to take part in any kinds of atrocities, no matter how difficult a situation they may end up in.

However, we have also seen that there may be good reasons not to be over-optimistic about this kind of pedagogical moral endeavour. If we want to feel certain that the kinds of atrocities we know from the past will not be repeated in the future, we had better try to identify which kinds they are. In addition, we ought to try to identify those wrongs that go relatively unnoticed in our own time. We should then try to make society a place where we are free of these kinds of atrocities, without requiring from the ordinary citizen too much virtue. For there is always a risk that, no matter how much zeal we put into the moral education of our children, if tempted, our children will forget all that they have learnt. This is perhaps the main moral lesson to be learnt from history.

Further reading about virtue ethics

Aristotle's main ethical writing is *Nicomachean Ethics* (Indianapolis, IN: Hackett, 1999). Alasdair MacIntyre's *After Virtue* (London: Duckworth, 1985) is a modern classic. Two anthologies with contributions to virtue ethics are David Slatman (ed.), *Virtue Ethics: A Critical Reader* (Edinburgh: Edinburgh University Press, 1997) and Roger Crisp and Michael Slote (eds), *Virtue Ethics* (Oxford: Oxford University Press, 1997). The articles quoted from Anscombe, Foot, Hursthouse and Slote are included in the latter anthology. Rosalind Hursthouse has developed her argument in *On Virtue Ethics* (Oxford: Oxford University Press, 1999) and there are also recent books by Philippa Foot, *Natural Goodness* (Oxford: Clarendon Press, 2001) and Michael Slote, *Morals from Motives* (Oxford: Oxford University Press, 2001). Criticisms of virtue ethics from the perspective of situationist psychology have been put forward by Gilbert Harman, for example, in 'The Nonexistence of Character Traits', *Proceedings of the Aristotelian Society,* vol. 100, 2000, p. 2236, and by J. M. Doris in 'Persons, Situations, and Virtue Ethics', *Nous*, vol. 32, 1998, pp. 504–30.

7

Feminist Ethics

Women and moral philosophy

Historically speaking, women have been largely absent from Western philosophy. There exists at least one exception in antiquity, however, the tragic figure of Hypatia (*c.* 370–415), a Neoplatonist philosopher and mathematician who was murdered when Cyril, the patriarch of Alexandria, had a Christian mob drag her to a church, where his monks excoriated her using oyster shells. But it is not until the eighteenth century that we meet with a name such as Mary Wollstonecraft (1759–97), with her strong defence of women's rights, and it is not until the twentieth century that women enter the philosophical stage *en masse*. The situation in moral philosophy is not very different from the situation in philosophy in general. And even if many women have entered philosophy during the last century, there are still, in most countries, many more male than female philosophers. Those who keep an eye on such things must have noted, however, that in the last chapter, where virtue ethics was discussed, the majority of the philosophers quoted and discussed were women. This does not mean that virtue ethics is exclusively a zone for female philosophers, but there is no denying that the proportion of female philosophers in this field is relatively high. Is this a mere coincidence, to be explained by the fact that when women entered moral philosophy virtue ethics happened to be in vogue, or does virtue ethics appeal in any special way to female thinkers? This is a controversial issue to which I will return. It must suffice for now to note that, nowadays, female philosophers play a role in all fields of philosophy in general, and in moral philosophy in particular. The trolley example, presented in the opening chapter of this book, and to which I have returned several times, has been formulated and elaborated upon by two distinguished female philosophers, Philippa Foot from the UK (defending virtue ethics) and Judith Jarvis Thomson from the USA (defending a moral rights view) respectively. As a matter of fact there are distinguished female philosophers defending each of the theories discussed so far in this book. To mention just a few examples: the Australian utilitarian philosopher Helga Kuhse, the deontological philosophers Christine M. Korsgaard (USA) and Onora O'Neill (UK) and, once again, the moral rights theorist Judith Jarvis Thomson (USA). Some of these philosophers may think of themselves as feminists, but their basic contributions to respective philosophy does not strike the reader as very different from the corresponding contributions made by male philosophers. Yet, it is worth pondering whether there is any such thing as a special female contribution to normative ethics. In that case, what does it amount to? Does it contribute any new moral insights? Can it, in its own right, enter the competition between utilitarianism, egoism, deontological ethics and the theory of rights and provide another criterion of right action? Or should it be conceived in line with how we eventually came to see virtue ethics, that is, as a complement, rather than as an alternative, to such more principled stances? These are questions to be discussed in the present chapter.

Before I enter into this discussion, just a few words on sexual prejudice in the history of Western philosophy.

Sexual prejudice within philosophy

The classical Greek philosopher and best-known advocate of virtue ethics, Aristotle, not only and famously put forward a principled defence of slavery, he also thought that women should play a very special role in society. And the reason was in both cases *natural difference*. He wrote as follows, in opposition to another, equally well-known Athenian philosopher, Socrates:

> [M]oral virtue belongs to all of them; but the temperance of a man and of a woman, or the courage and justice of a man and of a woman, are not, as Socrates maintained, the same; the courage of a man is shown in commanding, of a woman in obeying ... as the poet says of women, 'Silence is a woman's glory', but this is not equally the glory of man. (*Politics*, Book I:13)

This is only the beginning of a long tradition of prejudice against women, where some of the most important representatives are the famous Swiss Enlightenment philosopher Jean-Jacques Rousseau (1712–78) and Immanuel Kant. What is characteristic of a true woman, then, according to Rousseau? Well, she should certainly not be brilliant. 'A brilliant wife is a plague to her husband, her children, her friends, her valets, everyone,' he claimed. On the other hand, a woman who had developed her distinctively female traits was only a 'little lower than the angels'. Rousseau did not deny that women are capable of reasoning, but their reasoning is complementary, and ultimately subordinate, to that of men. A woman's reason, Rousseau wrote, is practical, attuned to detail and basically unprincipled. A man's reason, on the other hand, is abstract, general and principled. When applying this general view of the reason of women to normative ethics, the subject of this book, Rousseau arrived at the following conclusion:

> The search for abstract and speculative truth, for principles and axioms of science, for all that tends to wide generalisation, is beyond a woman's grasp; their studies should be thoroughly practical. It is their business to apply the principles discovered by men, it is their place to make the observations which lead men to discover those principles ... Woman should discover, so to speak, an experimental morality, man should reduce it to a system ... woman observes, man reasons. (*Emile*, pp. 340, 349, 350)

Kant adopted a similar position. While women had 'just as much understanding as the male', it was not a '*deep understanding*'. Her philosophy, Kant claimed, '... is not to reason but to sense', and women, according to Kant,

> will need to know nothing more of the cosmos than is necessary to make the appearance of the heavens on a beautiful evening a stimulating sight to them. ('On the Distinction of the Beautiful and Sublime in the Interrelations of the Two Sexes', p. 194)

A contrasting picture can be presented, however. Socrates and Plato (who wrote the dialogues with Socrates as the protagonist), as we have noted, thought that the same virtues applied to women and men. And Mary Wollstonecraft, who wrote *A Vindication of the Rights of Woman* (1792) as a response to Rousseau's *Emile*, argued explicitly that 'the nature of reason must be the same in all' (p. 42). Today we can only too easily distance ourselves from all these prejudices once they have been exposed. But does this mean that we ought to side with Wollstonecraft? This is not obvious. It may be fruitful here to distinguish between four possible reactions.

One reaction would be to claim that men and women should go on pursuing different approaches in ethics (that way, arguably, we have the best of both worlds). A second reaction would be that women should give up their traditional approach to moral problems and try to acquire what has typically been conceived of as a male approach to ethics. A third reaction would be to claim that men ought to give up their approach to moral philosophy and try to adopt what has typically been conceived of as a feminine approach. Finally, a fourth, more neutral stance to take up would be to claim that women and men alike should develop and combine both kinds of approaches.

The first reaction is hard to take seriously. How sad if men and women could not work side by side in moral philosophy! The second does not strike me as plausible either. What would become of moral philosophy if no concern were shown for practical questions? At least, such a reaction would be completely at variance with the very spirit of this book. Unless abstract moral reasoning has something to contribute to applied and practical ethics there is little point in pursuing it, I have argued. The fourth reaction, on the other hand, may seem to come to something of a platitude. Is it not the obvious solution? Should not both men and women try to escape the stereotypical views and enter each other's traditional field? Should not women take part in the principled discussion traditionally pursued within normative ethics? And should not men take part in practical ethics, articulating a stance on questions about abortion, euthanasia, our responsibility with respect to famine, environmental problems, and so forth?

Well, I must admit that I tend towards this fourth reaction. Note, however, that even the third reaction has had many recent advocates. According to them, there is something inherently problematic with the traditional male principled approach to moral problems. Men ought therefore to learn from women. Together, women and men ought to work out an alternative to the traditional approaches.

In the present context it is natural to concentrate on philosophers who tend to this third reaction. If they are right, we may be allowed to see feminist ethics as an alternative to more traditional approaches such as utilitarianism, egoism, deontological ethics, the theory of moral rights and virtue ethics (as traditionally worked out).

According to this third reaction, then, there may be a grain of truth in what Rousseau and Kant had to say about a typically female approach to ethics. This does not mean that Rousseau and Kant did not hold a prejudiced view of female moral thinking. But their mistake did not lie in their image of typically female ethical thinking; their mistake was rather their belief that the typically female approach to morality had nothing to teach male philosophers. In the rest of this chapter I will discuss views of this variety, that is, views claiming that there exists a typically female approach to ethical problems and that this approach should be conceived of as an alternative to a more traditional, male approach.

Carol Gilligan and the ethics of care

Until the end of the 1960s most people who advocated equal rights for women and men tended to believe that gender issues were of no relevance from a strictly philosophical point of view. With respect to moral philosophy they tended towards what I have characterised above as the fourth reaction. However, since then many feminist philosophers have come to question the assumption that philosophy in general, and moral philosophy in particular, is gender-neutral. What has been called a feminist, or feminine, ethics of care has been put forward as an alternative to traditional moral theories. This new interest in gender issues within moral philosophy originated in the work by the American psychologist Carol Gilligan. Gilligan has studied the moral development of children, and in her book *In a Different Voice* (1982) she claims that a result of her studies is that two different moral 'languages' exist, a language of impartiality or 'justice' and a relational language of 'care'. The 'different voice', that of care, was mainly associated with women. This was found as an empirical observation, she claims:

> The different voice I describe is characterized not by gender but theme. Its association with women is an empirical observation and it is primarily through women's voices that I trace its development. But this association is not absolute, and the contrasts between male and

female voices are presented here to highlight a distinction between two modes of thought ... rather than to represent a generalization about either sex. (*In a Different Voice*, p. 2)

The point of departure of Gilligan's study was the work by the educational psychologist Lawrence Kohlberg. Kohlberg had claimed that children go through a definite series of stages in their moral development. They start out at an egoistic level, go through a level where the individual conforms to stereotypical roles and conventional standards, and continue eventually to a level where moral principles are based on universal and impartial principles of justice. (Kohlberg actually distinguishes six different levels, but there is no need to go into detail here.) Kohlberg's theory had its empirical basis in a study of eighty-four boys, whose development he had followed for more than twenty years. His study was followed up with studies involving girls as well, and it then transpired that women did not, on average, achieve as high a standard of moral reasoning as men did. Women seemed on average to be less morally mature then men! This assumption was challenged by Gilligan, who claimed that, rather than being immature, women are just different. There exists an alternative female way of moral reasoning.

What, then, characterises the typically female moral approach? Obviously, according to Gilligan, it is not based on impartial principles of justice, but on care and responsibility within personal relationships. One example constructed by Kohlberg, and famously commented upon by Gilligan, is known as 'Heinz's Dilemma': a man named Heinz needs a drug to save his wife's life. The drug is expensive and Heinz cannot afford to buy it. The druggist refuses to reduce the price and so Heinz instead contemplates whether to steal the drug or not. The dilemma was presented to an eleven-year-old boy, Jake, and to an eleven-year-old girl, Amy.

Listen first to Jake's voice:

Jake: For one thing, a human life is worth more than money, and if the druggist only makes $1000, he is still going to live, but if Heinz doesn't steal the drug, his wife is going to die.
Question: Why is life worth more than money?
Jake: Because the druggist can get a thousand dollars later from rich people with cancer, but Heinz can't get his wife again.
Question: Why not?

Jake: Because people are all different and so you couldn't get Heinz's wife again.

This is contrasted with Amy's voice. Asked whether Heinz should steal the drug she answers:

> Well, I don't think so. I think there might be other ways besides stealing it, like if he could borrow the money or make a loan or something, but he really shouldn't steal the drug – but his wife shouldn't die either.

According to Kohlberg, it seems as if Jake has advanced beyond Amy in his moral development. Gilligan does not accept this conclusion. According to Gilligan, Jake saw the dilemma as if it were a mathematical problem. And since the solution is rationally derived, once the principles involved (concerning life and property respectively) are ranked, Jake assumes that anybody who thinks rationally about the question would arrive at the same conclusion. Amy, on the other hand, sees the problem as 'a narrative of relationships that extends over time'. Her world 'is a world of relationships and psychological truths where the awareness of the connection between people gives rise to a recognition of responsibility for one another, a perception of the need for response'. Her response is not less mature. It is just different.

Gilligan claims that her observation about this example can be generalised. Several other studies point in the same direction, she claims. There exists a certain way of approaching moral problems exhibited by many (but not all) women and by very few men, which can be characterised, in short, as an ethics of care:

> From a justice perspective, the self as moral agent stands as the figure against a ground of social relationships, judging the conflicting claims of self and others against a standard of equality or equal respect (the Categorical Imperative, the Golden Rule). From a care perspective, the relationship becomes the figure, defining self and others. Within the context of relationship, the self as a moral agent perceives and responds to the perception of need. The shift in moral perspective is manifest by a change in the moral question from 'What is just?' to 'How to respond?' ('Moral Orientation and Moral Development', p. 23)

Is her observation correct? In that case, what conclusions are we entitled to draw from it?

What can we learn from Gilligan's studies?

It is highly debatable what conclusions we should draw from Gilligan's studies. Do they really show that women and men on average approach moral problems differently? If they do, how are we to explain the difference? Can it be explained in biological terms, or is it brought about by differences in the way boys and girls are educated? If there is a difference, does it appear as Gilligan claims? Could we not explain the difference between Jake and Amy differently? Could we not say that, while Jake argues in deontological ethical terms, Amy takes a utilitarian approach? Listen to how Amy goes on to explain her reaction:

> If he stole the drug, he might save his wife then, but if he did, he might have to go to jail, and then his wife might get sick again, and he couldn't get more of the drug and it might not be good. So, they should really just talk it out and find some other way to make the money.

From a principled utilitarian point of view, is there anything to criticise in this argument?

All of this notwithstanding, let us for the sake of the argument assume that the difference Gilligan wants to emphasise exists (no matter how it can be explained). Let us assume that many women and few men tend to see a moral dilemma as 'a narrative of relationships that extends over time', and assume that the world of these women is a 'world of relationships and psychological truths where the awareness of the connection between people gives rise to a recognition of responsibility for one another, a perception of the need for response'. What significance has this from the point of view of normative ethics? In particular, is it possible to construct some kind of moral theory, a special ethics of care, in competition with traditional moral theories, which accounts for this other voice?

The ethics of care

Gilligan is not a philosopher and she has not attempted to work out any moral theory that could account in any systematic fashion for the special voice. The most influential example of such an attempt is Nel Noddings who, in her book *Caring: A Feminine Approach to Ethics and Moral Education* (1984), advocates a certain ethical theory that is indeed in competition with utilitarianism, egoism, deontological ethics and the theory of moral rights. Noddings criticises the traditional 'approach of the father', which she distinguishes from the 'approach of the mother'. The latter she identifies with a certain ethics of care.

> The first moves immediately to abstraction where ... thinking can take place clearly and logically in isolation from the complicating factors of particular persons, places, and circumstances; the second moves to concretization where ... feelings can be modified by the introduction of facts, the feelings of others, and personal histories. (*Caring*, pp. 36–7)

This is not very instructive. I suppose even a utilitarian or ethical egoist can agree with what has here been described as the 'approach of the mother'. However, when Noddings goes on to state her own criterion of rightness, it is obvious that she is in competition with traditional moral theories. According to Noddings, a decision is

> right or wrong according to how faithfully it was rooted in caring – that is, in a genuine response to the perceived needs of others. (*Caring*, p. 53)

This is obviously virtue ethics of a kind that Slote has called 'agent-based' (see the previous chapter about this). But this means that the same kind of objections that were discussed in the chapter on virtue ethics reappear.

In the first place, this *exclusive* focus on the agent may seem strange. Must not the reason that the action is right or wrong have *something* to do with what happens to those who are affected by it? This is a question that will be raised at least by utilitarians, egoists and moral rights theorists alike.

Second, is it not strange that only caring persons can perform right actions? After all, should not morality have something that can inform even those of us who are seriously deficient in terms of virtue (caring)? But if a caring character is a right-making characteristic, and lack of caring a wrong-making characteristic, then there is no way that a vicious person can act rightly.

Finally, even this version of virtue ethics has the strange implication that whatever action a caring person might perform (even a horrendous action) would be right.

In addition to this there are moral problems with Noddings' precise version of her agent-based virtue ethics. According to

Slote, a virtuous person is a benevolent person (in general). According to Noddings, a virtuous person is characterised by partiality. We have learnt from the discussion of utilitarianism in Chapter 2 that when dealing with those who are near and dear, some degree of partiality may be a good thing to exhibit, but is there no limit to this? According to Noddings there is such a limit, but the way she draws it is controversial. We cannot adopt an attitude of caring in relation to people who are starving in poor countries far away from us, Noddings notes. But this means that we need not concern ourselves with their suffering. Moreover, our caring relation to those who are near and dear to us may blind us to their faults. Noddings is very explicit on this point. She illustrates it with the following, often quoted, anecdote concerning Ms A, at the height of the civil rights movement in the USA:

> A problem concerning the rights and education of blacks arose, and the only black student in class spoke eloquently of the prevailing injustice and inhumanity against blacks, of his growing despair. He spoke of 'going to the barricade.' Ms A was nearly moved to tears. He was clearly right in condemning the treatment of his people and in demanding something better ... [Ms A said, I] 'could not – ever – oppose my bigoted old father or my hysterical Aunt Phoebe! ... Oh, she is wrong, and my father is wrong. But there are years of personal kindness. They must count for something ... I know I could not fight – really fight on the other side. And what now of the black man, Jim, who is, after all, 'right'? If my sights picked him out ... I would note that it was Jim and pass on to some other target. (*Caring*, pp. 109–10)

Noddings notes that there is a limit to this kind of partiality. Most of us would not care for a person who worked as a torturer in Auschwitz, she submits. However, *the limit is set by the person caring for the other*, showing a 'characteristic variability in her actions'. This person may ponder how far she is prepared to go, but there is no way for her to search for an answer in any independent principle. This means that there is really no way to go too far in one's caring for those who are near and dear, and in one's corresponding complacency with respect to the suffering of others. The extremes to which you are prepared to go determine your morally permissible limits! This is hard to accept.

A caring disposition

The best way of understanding an ethics of care is perhaps not to take it to state a criterion of rightness. Why not think of a caring disposition as a disposition that tends to help us solve hard practical questions, or as a disposition guarding us against too evil actions, by analogy with how we conceived of virtue ethics in the preceding chapter?

There is something to recommend such an understanding. There is no doubt that the caring attitude has been neglected when the traditional lists of the virtues have been drawn up. This is at least true if we consider lists of virtues thought to be suited to men. When we look at the lists of typically feminine virtues, such as the ones put forward by Aristotle, Rousseau or Kant, the situation is different. We here find something remarkably close to modern versions of the ethics of care. According to these thinkers, women should develop a caring disposition. But we have already noted that Aristotle, Rousseau and Kant held prejudices against women. Their prejudices surfaced when they claimed that these virtues suit women exclusively. According to the most plausible interpretation of the ethics of care, it seems to me, it should be urged, rather, that everybody – male and female – should exhibit a caring disposition alike. At least this seems to be a necessity in a society where gender stereotypes are tending to erode. And I suppose that most readers of this book belong to such societies. Men are becoming increasingly responsible for the care of their children as well as being breadwinners, while women are becoming breadwinners as well as being mothers.

What is characteristic of a moral expert who is good at solving hard practical problems? We have assumed that two kinds of expertise are of importance. A moral expert (wise person) must have a grasp of general moral truths that may be of importance in the concrete case. And the moral expert (wise person) must be good at getting a grasp of all the facts in the situation that may be relevant to the solution of the problem at hand. It is very plausible to argue that a caring disposition may be of importance in both ways.

Take first the discussion about what general moral truths may be of importance in the concrete case. Unless one has developed a tendency to care for others, it is hardly likely that one will understand the true moral importance of relations of care. The objection to utilitarianism, that it does not take such relations seriously, would never have been put forward, I submit, had there not been moral philosophers with their own experience of caring. And a utilitarian with no experience of care would be at a loss when discussing this objection. It is even more obvious that it must often be impossible to grasp all the facts that are relevant to the solution to a hard practical problem unless one has some personal experience of caring for others. After all, caring relations matter to people involved in most practical cases, so there is no solution to the problem unless one finds a reasonable way of paying due respect to these relations. Once again, I submit, no one who has not personally experienced caring relations can understand what such relations really amount to.

Is it also true that a capacity to care for others may be a safeguard against immoral action? It is certainly true that a capacity to care for those who are near and dear may prevent us from selfishly pursuing our own interests at the cost of theirs. A caring parent is prepared to make sacrifices in the interest of his or her children. A caring parent does not treat his or her children badly, at least not deliberately. However, there is another side to this coin. A caring relationship with those who are near and dear may come to mean that we treat other people badly. Out of concern for those who are near and dear to us, we may treat others with complacency or even with cruelty. Our caring relationship with some people may blind us to the fact that, in our concern for their interests, we hurt those who are not near and dear to us (in a way a utilitarian could not accept), or violate their rights (if such a thing as rights exists), or disregard certain absolute moral prohibitions (if such prohibitions exist).

The obvious remedy to this danger, however, would be not to give up one's disposition to care, but to try to develop a well-rounded moral character, where virtues such as justice and benevolence are no less important than the disposition to care.

A radical feminist critique

What has been said so far may appear to some much too conciliatory. If my argument is correct, there is no such thing as a plausible feminist ethics of care in competition with utilitarianism, egoism, deontological ethics and the ethics of moral rights. However, a disposition to care, stressed by many feminist moral philosophers, may be a complement to other moral virtues, of importance to both women and men who seek moral expertise (wisdom) and who want to guard themselves against certain kinds of evil action. If all this is correct, then the situation within moral philosophy may seem promising from the point of view of gender equality. Women are taking up the subject in large numbers; they are participating in the discussion about moral principles on equal terms with male philosophers. At the same time, many male philosophers have entered the field of applied or practical ethics, where they take part on equal terms with female philosophers. However, there exists a more radical feminist critique, which would reject the picture given here. According to this critique, what has here been described is rather, to use a term coined by the radical German-American philosopher Herbert Marcuse (1898–1979), a situation of successful male 'repressive tolerance'. Women have certainly been allowed to become involved in moral philosophy, these critics concede, but women have not been allowed to enter the subject on their own terms. Only those women who have accepted the traditional male way of doing moral philosophy have been acknowledged.

Let us look at this radical feminist critique. We saw aspects of it in Noddings' objection to 'abstraction' in moral philosophy:

> The first moves immediately to abstraction where ... thinking can take place clearly and logically in isolation from the complicating factors of particular persons, places, and circumstances; the second moves to concretization where ... feelings can be modified by the introduction of facts, the feelings of others, and personal histories. (*Caring*, pp. 36–7)

Gilligan also argues against too much trust in the use of hypothetical examples, of the kind that appear so frequently in a book like this one – it is irresistible to think here in particular about Philippa Foot's and Judith Jarvis Thomson's trolley examples:

> Hypothetical dilemmas, in the abstraction of their presentation, divest moral actors from the history and psychology of their individual lives and separate the moral problem from the social contingencies of its possible occurrence ... these dilemmas are useful for the distillation and refinement of objective principles of justice and for measuring the formal logic of equality and reciprocity. However, the reconstruction of the dilemma in its contextual particularity allows the understanding of cause and consequence which

engages the compassion and tolerance repeatedly noted to distinguish the moral judgement of women. (*In a Different Voice*, p. 100)

It is as if these authors take pride in what Rousseau claimed, that 'the search for abstract and speculative truth, for principles and axioms of science, for all that tends to wide generalisation, is beyond a woman's grasp'. And they go on to argue that the typically female approach to moral problems is the only sound approach to take up.

A general statement of this position can be found in the work of distinguished feminist philosopher Alison Jaggar, who defines something she calls a 'Feminist Practical Discourse' (FPD):

1. FPD typically does not begin with the articulation of general moral principles but instead begins with the creation of opportunities for participants to talk about their own lives.
2. FPD requires that socially disempowered women be heard with special respect.
3. FPD emphasises the need to provide a supportive environment in which participants will feel safe enough to speak openly about their own lives.
4. FPD's most striking feature is that it is nurturant rather than adversarial.

How are we to respond to this radical feminist critique? I cannot help but feel that, once again, the only reasonable response must be conciliatory in nature. What is said here about the importance of facing moral dilemmas in all their concreteness seems to be perfectly reasonable as a *complement* to a more principled approach. And FPD, as described by Jaggar, may be of importance as a manner of preparing the way for a more traditional approach. In the final analysis, however, there is no way to solve moral dilemmas unless one is prepared to go through hard normative ethical thinking of the kind exemplified in this book.

Further reading about feminist ethics

Carol Gilligan, *In a Different Voice: Psychological Theory and Women's Development* (Cambridge, MA: Harvard University Press, 1982). The Heinz Dilemma is described in Lawrence Kohlberg, 'Stage and Sequence: The Cognitive Development Approach to Socialization', in D. A. Goslin (ed.), *Handbook of*

Socialization Theory and Research (Chicago: Rand-McNally, 1969), p. 379. Nel Noddings presents a feminine ethics of care in *Caring: A Feminine Approach to Ethics and Moral Education* (Berkeley: University of California Press, 1984). Anthologies discussing Carol Gilligan and the ethics of care are M. J. Larrabee (ed.), *An Ethic of Care* (London and New York: Routledge, 1993) and Virginia Held (ed.), *Feminist Morality: Transforming Culture, Society and Politics* (Chicago: Chicago University Press 1993). Gilligan's article 'Moral Orientation and Moral Development' is published in Eva Feder Kittay and Diana T. Meyers (eds), *Women and Moral Theory* (Totowa, NJ: Rowman and Littlefield, 1987), pp. 19–33. Many sexual prejudices in philosophy are exposed in Helga Kuhse's book on nursing ethics, *Caring: Nurses, Women, and Ethics* (Oxford: Blackwell, 1997). The quotation from Aristotle is from W. D. Ross (ed.), *The Works of Aristotle*, vol. 10 (Oxford: Clarendon Press, 1921). The quotation from Rousseau is from *Emile* (London: Dent, 1966). The quotation from Kant is from 'On the Distinction of the Beautiful and Sublime in the Interrelations of the Two Sexes', reprinted in Mary Briody Mahowald (ed.), *Philosophy of Woman* (Indianapolis, IN: Hackett, 1978), and the quotation from Mary Wollstonecraft has been taken from her *A Vindication of the Rights of Woman* (New York: Norton, 1967). The quotation from Jaggar is taken from Alison M. Jaggar, 'Feminist Ethics: Projects, Problems, Prospects', reprinted in Claudia Card (ed.), *Feminist Ethics* (Lawrence: University of Kansas Press, 1991), pp. 78–104. Alison M. Jaggar and Iris Young (eds), *A Companion to Feminist Philosophy* (Oxford: Blackwell, 1998) is a standard reference work.

8

Environmental Ethics

The expanding circle

Ironically enough, it seems as though the problem with global warming, which poses a threat to the very existence of the human race on earth, has meant that environmental problems proper have been eclipsed. The focus on human interests and human interests only has been reinforced. And yet if there are ecological values not reducible to human interests, even these values are being put at risk through a possible future environmental disaster. So the reason to discuss them is still there. But are there moral concerns that are not reducible in some way or other to human interests? This will be discussed in the present chapter.

Many of the moral theories presented in this book are extremely anthropocentric. This is true of egoism, of course, but also of some versions of utilitarianism, deontological ethics and the theory of moral rights (in its traditional version). Advocates of deontological ethics in particular have declared that animals lack moral standing. With Kant this is made clear with something close to brutality:

> But so far as animals are concerned, we have no direct duties. Animals ... are there merely as means to an end. That end is man. (*Lectures on Ethics*, p. 239)

And Aquinas had earlier made the same point as follows:

> Hereby is refuted the error of those who said it is sinful for a man to kill dumb animals: for by divine providence they are intended for man's use in the natural order. Hence it is no wrong for a man to make use of them, either by killing them or in any other way whatever. (*Summa Theologica*, II, II, Q. 64, Art. 6)

And the view can be traced back to Aristotle, who claimed that:

> after the birth of animals, plants exist for their sake, and that the
> other animals exist for the sake of man, the tame for use and food,
> the wild, if not all, at least the greater part of them, for food, and for
> the provision of clothing and various instruments. Now if nature
> makes nothing incomplete, and nothing in vain, the inference must
> be that she has made all animals for the sake of man. (*Politics*, Book
> I:9)

There are certainly religions, such as Buddhism and Hinduism,
that are far less anthropocentric than the Judeo-Christian
tradition but, within Western culture, the anthropocentric point
of departure went unchallenged for a very long time. However,
classical hedonistic utilitarianism, put forward by Jeremy
Bentham, meant a radical break with this tradition. This is what
Bentham had to say about the moral status of animals:

> The day *may* come when the rest of the animal creation may acquire
> those rights which never could have been witholden from them but
> by the hand of tyranny. The French have already discovered that
> the blackness of the skin is no reason why a human being should be
> abandoned without redress to the caprice of a tormentor. It may come
> one day to be recognized, that the number of the legs, the villosity of
> the skin, or the termination of the *os sacrum*, are reasons equally
> insufficient for abandoning a sensitive being to the same fate. What
> else is it that should trace the insuperable line? Is it the faculty of
> reason, or, perhaps, the faculty of discourse? But a full-grown horse
> or dog, is beyond comparison a more rational, as well as a more
> conversable animal, than an infant of a day or a week, or even a
> month, old. But suppose the case were otherwise, what would it
> avail? The question is not, Can they *reason*? nor, Can they *talk*? but,
> Can they *suffer*? (*Principles of Morals and Legislation*, p. 283)

Bentham's defence of the moral status of animals was not
unprecedented. In antiquity, Zeno and some Stoics defended
vegetarianism, and one of the founders of Neoplatonism,
Porphyry (who lived between 232 and some time in the first six
years of the fourth century), took up a position similar to
Bentham's:

> To compare plants, however, with animals, is doing violence to the
> order of things. For the latter are naturally sensitive, and adapted to
> feel pain, to be terrified and hurt. But the former are entirely destitute
> of sensation, and in consequence of this, nothing foreign, or evil, or

hurtful, or injurious, can befall them. For sensation is the principle of all alliance. (*On Abstinence from Animal Food*, III:19)

The contemporary preference utilitarian Peter Singer, who has argued that sentient animals are in many ways of equal moral stature to people, has taken up the theme. Even animals have interests, according to Singer; if they can suffer or experience pleasure, then they have interests, and these interests are no less important than corresponding interests held by humans. There is a difference, however, between adult human beings and many animals. With the possible exception of certain mammals, even those animals that can feel pleasure and pain do not conceive of themselves as individuals existing in time, with a past, a present and a future. This means that if we kill them, while we rob them of possible future satisfaction of preferences, we do not violate their interest in continued life. They lack such an interest. So while adult human beings and some mammals have a direct interest in continued life, the interest most animals have in continued life is merely indirect.

Personally I am not convinced by this argument. Even a preference utilitarian should conceive of our interest in future life as mainly indirect. First of all, is it true that we hold an intrinsic preference for continued life? I am not so sure. If we want to go on with our lives, this is because we believe that continued life will give us satisfaction of more basic preferences, such as preferences for pleasure, or knowledge, or achievements, and so forth. And even if we were to have an intrinsic preference for continued life, is it really violated when we are killed? After all, when we are killed we also lose the preference for continued life. So there is no time when we have this preference and it is not satisfied. When we have the preference, it is not yet frustrated, and when it is frustrated, we no longer have it. I have already touched upon the problem of how a preference utilitarian ought to handle preferences no longer held by a person, and I will not pursue the subject any further here. It should suffice here to note that even if Singer accepts a principled difference between (most) human beings and (most) other animals, he ends up with an even more radical conclusion than Bentham did. According to Bentham it is acceptable to raise animals for food, provided we are kind to them. Singer defends vegetarianism, and his book *Animal Liberation* has been enormously influential for a movement defending the interests of sentient animals in our time.

We have also seen that some attempts have been made to revise the theory of moral rights, most famously by Tom Regan in his book *The Case for Animal Rights*, so that it can acknowledge that some animals are moral subjects, possessing moral rights,

It has seemed to many contemporary thinkers as if old prejudices held with respect to animals will eventually decay. According to these thinkers, our moral reasoning now provides us with an 'expanding circle' (the title of a book by Singer). But where is the expansion to end? Note that Aristotle thought that plants exist for the sake of animals. Was that a prejudice too? Must we also include plants in our moral concern? This is what some critics of utilitarianism and theories of animal rights have claimed. These approaches are on the right track, they concede, but they do not go far enough. Nature itself has intrinsic value and must be taken into account. Theories to this effect will be discussed in the present chapter.

Do natural environments have value in themselves?

There exists an extensive interest in environmental questions in our age, which takes as its point of departure an interest in human welfare (or perhaps the welfare of humans and other sentient beings). It is not difficult to acknowledge that certain kinds of natural disasters may come to harm human and other sentient beings as well. Global warming is what first comes to mind. This is why 'sustainable' development is sought. Even a utilitarian must conceive of global warming and pollution of our atmosphere and oceans as possible threats to future welfare. However, there is a limit to how a utilitarian can defend a natural order. Note that, according to utilitarianism as classically conceived, there are two ways of making the world a better place. One is to make existing individuals happier; the other is to make (additional) happy individuals. And note, furthermore, that if we want to maximise welfare, it may well be that, in order to do so, we must opt for an enormous population, where each individual leads a life barely worth living, rather than a more restricted population where everybody is very happy (the loss in quality is compensated for by a larger gain in quantity). This conclusion of classical utilitarian thinking has been dubbed 'the repugnant conclusion' by the Oxford philosopher Derek Parfit. However, utilitarians (such as the present author) tend to defend this conclusion and claim that the name Parfit has given it is a misnomer.

Be that as it may, it is clear that classical utilitarianism has this implication and this means that classical hedonistic utilitarianism may be hard to reconcile with certain strands of environmental ethical thinking. Sustainable development, measured from the point of view of utilitarianism, may well have effects at variance with what some adherents of a more principled environmental ethics are prepared to accept. They may want a *principled* defence for the preservation of nature. Here such principled defences of the environment will be discussed. I am thinking of arguments to the effect that natural environments, such as rainforests, woods near mountain tops or ecosystems ought to be preserved because they possess value in themselves. I am also thinking of arguments to the effect that existing species should be preserved, because this is considered to be of value in itself. Or there are ideas to the effect that a rich and complex diversity of species should be maintained because this is considered to be of value in itself. And I am thinking finally of such grandiose ideas as the 'Gaia hypothesis', put forward by the ecologist James Lovelock. According to the Gaia hypothesis, the entire biosphere can be seen as a living, self-regulating and self-preserving organism, of value in itself.

Are any such views plausible? We may speak of them somewhat loosely as examples of 'deep' ecological thinking (the term has been coined by the Oslo philosopher Arne Naess). Note that the implications of these ideas may be very far-reaching. On an ecological platform, Naess states:

> The flourishing of human life and cultures is compatible with a substantial decrease of the human population. The flourishing of nonhuman life requires such a decrease. ('The Deep Ecological Movement', p. 14)

And, in a comment to this principle, it is said that:

> Estimates of an optimal human population vary. Some quantitative estimates are 100 million, 500 million, and 1000 million, but it is recognized that there must be a long range, humane reduction through mild but tenacious political and economic measures. This will make possible, as a result of increased habitat, population

growth for thousands of species which are now constrained by human pressures. (Ibid., pp. 19–20)

Consequentialism, deontology, or a theory of rights?

Many of those who have defended deep ecology have not been philosophers, let alone moral philosophers. They have rarely been clear about the exact nature of their moral positions. Some of them have argued that certain values, such as nature untouched by humans, or characterised by ecological diversity and complexity, should be *maximised*. Others have tended towards deontological ethics and claimed that there are certain limits to what we are permitted to do. Humankind should not play God and, for example, wipe out, or create new, species. Others have claimed that entities such as old and impressive mountains can have certain *rights* to protection. And there exist both environmental virtue ethics and environmental feminist ethics (ecofeminism).

I will not try to separate these approaches from each other. The reader is well versed by now in this terminology and can easily cast the deep ecological ethical thoughts in his or her favoured form. The focus here will be on the specific value assumptions put forward by ecological thinkers, whether in consequentialist, deontological or moral rights terms: is it true that nature, or certain natural environments, ought to be preserved? Is it true that nature should be preserved *for its own sake*?

Arguments in defence of deep ecology

If we want to defend a particular version of environmental ethics, or a particular form of deep ecology, we have to give a precise account of what it is that we see as valuable in itself. If we say that 'nature' ought to be preserved, then we have to distinguish nature from something else, such as culture, before we go on to say what makes it special from a moral point of view. If we say that a complex and harmonious diversity of many species is of importance, we have to say something about how to measure complexity, harmony and diversity among species. And, in particular, we have to give a clear definition of the very notion of a species. I will not go into such problems here. There is no denying that such questions can be answered. They can be answered in many different ways and the result will be more or less plausible versions of deep ecology. The question I want to discuss here is a more radical one: is there *any* such version of deep ecology that results in a plausible version of environmental ethics?

This discussion can be pursued in very general terms. Let us assume that some kind of 'organic whole' has been identified, such as a certain mountain, or a species, or a complex of species, or an ecosystem, or a complex of ecosystems, or the entire biosphere, or what have you; the question I want to discuss is what kind of arguments can be given for and against the idea that (the preservation of) such an organic whole may be of value in itself.

It should be noted that some kinds of environmental ethics are of a form very similar to political conservatism. What they amount to is a certain attitude. Some existing natural environments should be preserved, not because they can be shown in any direct way to be of value, but because they have come to exist the way they have, it is argued. What has come about or evolved in a certain way ought to be preserved, period. For example, we ought not to drive to extinction species that have through a natural process become part of the natural order, and we ought not to add through genetic manipulation new species to the natural order. But are there any arguments in defence of such a very general conservative attitude? Of course there are. Some of them are pragmatic in nature, others are more principled.

One argument for the conservative attitude would be to say that if we eradicate species or add new ones to the natural order, then we are playing God. If we do, we transgress a moral limit. This can be taken literally. After all, according to Genesis, God created the species (including *Homo sapiens*) and he ordained us to hold dominion over the other species, not to wipe them out or add new ones to his creation:

> And God said, Let us make man in our image, after our likeness: and let them have dominion over the fish of the sea, and over the fowl of the air, and over the earth, and over every creeping thing that creepeth upon the earth.
> So God created man in his own image, in the image of God created he him; male and female created he them.
> And God blessed them, and God said unto them, be fruitful and multiply, and replenish the earth, and subdue it; and have dominion over the fish of the sea, and over the fowl of the air, and over every

living thing that moveth upon the earth. (Genesis 1:24–8, Authorised Version)

We saw, however, in the introductory chapter to this book, that such a reference does not settle the matter of whether we are allowed to wipe out species or create new ones. And the main problem with this line of argument is not that according to modern science God did not, once and for all, create the species. They have evolved slowly, over millions of years. The person who wants to take up the conservative stance with respect to nature may just revise the account narrated. He or she can still insist that God has created the species, only indirectly, via a mechanism of chance variation and natural selection. The result is still sacrosanct, according to this argument. But a problem remains. How do we know that God's creation deserves to be preserved? That God told us so will not be taken as an answer. For how do we know this? How do we know that Genesis was not dictated by Satan? We know this only if we compare the message sent with our own considered moral judgement. Only if the message sent is decent are we allowed to assume that it originates with an infinitely good being. So we are still left with the problem: why not eliminate species and why not create new ones through genetic engineering?

Why not then defend the existing and natural order of species with reference to the wisdom of evolution? After all, this is how many political conservatives have defended well-established and existing social institutions. The argument, however, is problematic in both fields. First of all, it is merely pragmatic in nature. So it does not really provide the foundation of a principled defence of the existing order. Moreover, evolution itself has often brought about all sorts of natural (and social) disasters. So even if there is much truth in the belief that we should be very cautious before we make far-reaching interventions in the natural order since the consequences may be far-reaching as well and difficult to assess *ex ante*, there may be clear cases where the advantages of making the kind of changes seem, from a pragmatic point of view, irresistible. What if we find that we have to wipe out certain species in order not be wiped out ourselves? Who then would not be prepared to intervene in the natural evolutionary process?

An alternative line of argument would be if it could be shown that the organic whole one sets out to defend has a spirit. Again, we find this line of argument within some brands of political conservatism. The preservation of the nation, or the cultural or ethnic community, is defended with the argument that it has a personality and a will too. And if it has, it is only natural to pay due respect to it. This line has often been taken up not only by representatives of an idealistic German philosophical tradition, but also by the contemporary British conservative philosopher Roger Scruton:

> [S]ociety is more than a speechless organism. It has a personality and a will. Its history, institutions and culture are the repositories of human values – in short, it has the character of end as well as means. (*The Meaning of Conservatism*, p. 23)

The most spectacular application of this line of reasoning within environmental ethics would be to apply it to the biosphere as such. This would mean that even a hedonistic utilitarian would have to expand the circle of moral concern to include the biosphere. Actually, there exists one hedonistic utilitarian who has taken up this stance in his defence of deep ecology, the Scottish moral philosopher Timothy Sprigge.

The argument does not strike me as convincing. Already the Gaia hypothesis is very speculative. Why conceive of the biosphere as an organism? And even if we do, why believe that it is sentient? And even if we do believe that the biosphere is a sentient organism, what practical conclusions are we to draw from this belief? How do we know when we hurt this organism? If we eradicate a certain rainforest, say, how do we know that we are hurting the biosphere? Perhaps the biosphere enjoys what we are doing. Perhaps the biosphere was more uncomfortable before than after our intervention. Perhaps it feels the way I do after I have shaved. Who is to say? Well, the biosphere itself, one may want to answer. But as far as I know, the biosphere does not speak to us. And if it did, who would be able to understand the message?

Aesthetic value

The term 'organic whole', and ideas to the effect that a 'complex' and 'harmonious' diversity of many species should be preserved, invite an aesthetic understanding of deep ecology. Why not argue in defence of some natural organic whole, not with reference to any assumption that it is conscious, but rather with reference to the putative fact that it is beautiful? Or, if the term 'beautiful' has perhaps lost much of its appeal in a postmodern society, why not argue in defence of the natural organic whole with direct reference to the putative fact that it has value in itself; after all, many people believe that certain pieces of art have value in themselves, without claiming that they are beautiful. Why not then assume that this holds true also, and perhaps to a much greater extent, of certain natural organic wholes?

The Cambridge philosopher G. E. Moore (1873–1958) famously defended the view that certain organic wholes have intrinsic value. He addressed the question from the point of view of nature and culture alike. According to Moore, some pieces of art have intrinsic value, but so have certain 'natural' organic wholes. As a matter of fact, when giving his most often quoted example of an organic whole with (aesthetic) intrinsic value, he speaks of nature:

> Let us imagine one world exceedingly beautiful. Imagine it as beautiful as you can; put into it whatever on this earth you most admire – mountains, rivers, the sea; trees, and sunsets, stars and moon. Imagine these all combined in the most exquisite proportions, so that no one thing jars against another, but each contributes to increase the beauty of the whole. And then imagine the ugliest world you can possibly conceive. Imagine it simply one heap of filth, containing everything that is most disgusting to us, for whatever reason, and the whole, as far as may be, without one redeeming feature. Such a pair of worlds we are entitled to compare ... The only thing we are not entitled to imagine is that any human being ever has, or ever, by any possibility, can, live in either, can ever see and enjoy the beauty of the one or hate the foulness of the other. Well, even so, supposing them quite apart from any possible contemplation by human beings; still, is it irrational to hold that it is better that the beautiful world should exist, than the one which is ugly? Would it not be well, in any case, to do what we could to produce it rather than the other? Certainly I cannot help thinking that it would; and I hope that some may agree with me in this extreme instance. (*Principia Ethica*, pp. 83–4)

We can hear this kind of argument echo in many modern and postmodern defences of deep ecology. I do not think that Naess would reject an interpretation of his position along these lines.

Moore's argument is, of course, problematic. Is there any such thing as beauty that is not perceived? Well, the assumption that there is takes us some way into a problematic ontology, but perhaps not too far. So why not accept that the beauty is there, irrespective of whether it can be sensed or not? However, this only leads us to the next and crucial question. How can it be of any value if no one is there to appreciate it? The fact that Moore himself cannot help thinking that it has value does not show that it has value. Nor would it be of much avail if his hope that others will share his opinion were borne out by realities.

However, I think Moore is right when he insists that it is not *irrational* to hold that a beautiful world may be better than an ugly one. At least I am prepared to agree about this if an opinion, in order to be irrational, must be *confused* or *inconsistent* or something of the kind. And even if he has not given any positive argument in defence of the position that a beautiful world is better than an ugly one, he may well be right about this. Suppose he is. What practical conclusions are we to draw from this assumption? If mountains, rivers, the sea, trees and sunsets, stars and moon, combined in the most exquisite proportions, add up to a whole with intrinsic value, how important is this value as compared to other values?

Representatives of deep ecology have been bold when they have answered this question. They have not hesitated to pay a price in terms of welfare (brought about, for example, through the reduction of the number of sentient beings living on the earth) for the preservation of certain natural organic wholes. Moore himself was rather cautious. If the sum total of welfare was held constant, he preferred a beautiful world to an ugly one. However, he was not prepared to pay any price in terms of welfare, at least not in terms of deserved welfare, for the preservation of organic wholes of the kind discussed here. So the question remains to be answered: if a certain mountain has intrinsic value, what price are we prepared to pay (in terms of welfare) for its preservation?

Arguments against deep ecology

There is no convincing, knockdown argument in defence of deep ecology, but in this the position is no different from competing moral theories such as utilitarianism, egoism, deontological ethics (in their standard forms, paying no special interest to ecological values), or the traditional ethics of rights. Are there any strong arguments that can be put forward against it?

Two kinds of argument have often been put forward against the deep ecological position. One is methodological, the other ethical in nature. I will discuss them in order. According to the methodological objection already hinted at, the idea that organic wholes have intrinsic value must rest on an ontological mistake. Such things as organic wholes, 'collective' entities, do not really exist. And if they do not exist, it must be a mistake to believe that they possess intrinsic value.

It is true that according to deep ecology, collective entities such as species and complexes of species do exist. But is this belief really mistaken? Note that many of the moral theories discussed in this book assume that human individuals (persons) exist. According to egoism, each individual ought to maximise his or her welfare. And according to the theory of rights, each moral subject has moral rights. Are there individuals? Are there moral subjects? It is certainly true that, according to some philosophers, even individuals (persons) have a kind of fictitious existence. We are said to be 'bundles of experiences', or something of the kind. But it would be strange to argue against ethical egoism that the ego does not really exist. If egoism is a plausible moral view, then individuals *do* exist. For how do we know whether a certain entity exists or not? A plausible methodological rule of thumb is to assume that those (and only those) entities to which we have to make a reference in our best theories about the world exist. And here my submission is that our *moral* theories must be included as well. But then we cannot argue against egoism that individuals are fictitious entities, nor can we argue against deep ecology that species do not exist. We have to assess these respective views according to their moral merits. If we find that egoism is a plausible view, then we are allowed to conclude that individuals exist. If we find that deep ecology presents us with a plausible view, we have to admit that species, and systems of species, are real enough. We need no independent evidence to this effect.

But does deep ecology present us with a plausible moral position? Would it be a good idea to make sacrifices in terms of welfare in order, say, to save a species? Would it be right to kill individuals in order to save a species?

A telling example of this kind of conflict has been much discussed in Europe in the last few years, when the ruddy duck came to the attention of ornithologists. The late Sir Peter Scott's Wildfowl Trust at Slimbridge had introduced the ruddy duck to Europe from America. During the 1960s a handful escaped. The ruddy duck soon created havoc among Europe's duck populations. It spread from Britain and, defying normal laws of reproduction, mated with the white-headed duck so successfully that it was endangering the rare species in its native Spain and Turkey. In order to save the rare species, a controversial cull of ruddy ducks was launched in Britain, resulting in around 1,000 of the estimated 4,000 population being shot. This policy met with opposition from people supporting the rights of (individual) animals, who based their arguments on utilitarian or moral rights assumptions, but it met with approval from ornithologists and British conservationists, who based their moral arguments on deep ecological assumptions. Chris Mead, one of Britain's leading ornithologists, says, according to the *Evening Standard* (19 September 2000):

> I like ruddy ducks – in America. It's a great shame they have to be destroyed over here but I think it is the only way to save the white-headed duck as a different species.

Can this be a sound moral approach to adopt? Is it right to kill individuals in order to save a species?

Should we accept the deep ecological position?

We have seen that the deep ecological position can be defended along two different lines. On the one hand, there exists a traditional conservative and pragmatic defence of the position. According to this line of argument, we ought to be extremely cautious, for example, when we wipe out, or create new, species. On the other hand, there exists a line of argument taking its point of departure in the assumption that organic wholes such as species, or the entire biosphere, may be of value in themselves.

Both lines of argument are defensible but face both methodological and moral difficulties. In this, however, they are not very different from other moral theories discussed in this book. Note, however, that the practical implications of deep ecology may be very different, depending on which line of defence is adopted. If a conservative stance is taken up, we may find that we have to try to protect an existing and well-established natural order just to make sure that we do not put in jeopardy what evolution has achieved. This may tend to make us suspicious of rapid technological and scientific advances. If the point of departure is rather the idea that organic wholes have intrinsic value, we may find that we have good reasons also to *create* such wholes. Why not try, if a complex and harmonious diversity of many species is of such value, to establish such diversity all over the universe?

Is there life on Mars? Perhaps not, but in that case why not try to establish life there? Why not try to initiate an evolutionary process on Mars, leading to a situation where the desired diversity is a fact? This may well mean that we end up with an environmental ethics very sympathetic to science and technology.

Further reading about environmental ethics

Peter Singer's *Animal Liberation* (New York: Random House, 1975) is a classic statement of the view that sentient animals have interests that matter. The quotation from Porphyry is from *On Abstinence from Animal Food* (London: Centaur, 1965). The quotation from Aristotle is from W. D. Ross (ed.), *The Works of Aristotle*, vol. 10 (Oxford: Clarendon Press, 1921). The quotation from Aquinas can be found in *Basic Writings of Saint Thomas Aquinas*, vol. 1, edited by Anton C. Pegis (New York: Random House, 1945). The quotation from Bentham is from J. H. Burns and H. L. A. Hart (eds), *Principles of Morals and Legislation* (London: Methuen, 1982). Derek Parfit discusses 'the repugnant conclusion' in Part 4 of *Reasons and Persons* (Oxford: Clarendon Press, 1984). See also G. Arrhenius, J. Ryberg and T. Tännsjö, 'The Repugnant Conclusion', *Stanford Encyclopedia of Philosophy*. Timothy Sprigge puts forward his view in 'Are There Intrinsic Values in Nature?', *Journal of Applied Philosophy*, vol. 4, 1987. The Gaia hypothesis is put forward by James Lovelock in *Gaia – A New Look at Life on Earth* (Oxford: Oxford University Press, 1978). Arne Naess introduced the term 'deep ecology' in 'The Shallow and the Deep. Long-range Ecological Movement. A Summary', *Inquiry*, vol. 16, 1973, pp. 95–100. The quotation from Naess is from 'The Deep Ecological Movement: Some Philosophical Aspects', *Philosophical Inquiry*, vol. 8, 1986, pp. 10–31. The most elaborated statement of Naess's view is in Arne Naess, *Ecology, Community and*

Lifestyle: Outline of an Ecosophy (Cambridge: Cambridge University Press, 1989). Aldo Leopold was a pioneer for environmental ethics with the book *A Sand County Almanac and Sketches Here and There* (Oxford: Oxford University Press, 1949). My quotation from G. E. Moore is from *Principia Ethica* (Cambridge: Cambridge University Press, 1965). The methodological rule of thumb (about what to accept as real), stated at the end of this chapter, is a generalisation of an idea put forward by Gilbert Harman in *The Nature of Morality* (New York: Oxford University Press, 1977), ch. 1. Recent introductions to environmental ethics are John Benson, *Environmental Ethics: An Introduction with Readings* (London and New York: Routledge, 2000), Robert Eliot (ed.), *Environmental Ethics* (Oxford: Oxford University Press, 1995), Dale Jamieson (ed.), *A Companion to Environmental Philosophy* (Oxford: Blackwell, 2000), and Andrew Light and Holmes Rolston III (eds), *Environmental Ethics: An Anthology* (Oxford: Blackwell, 2003). A recent text about ecological integrity is Laura Westra et al. (eds), *Ecological Integrity: Integrating Environment, Conservation, and Health* (Washington, DC: Island Press, 2000).

9

What are we to Believe?

Conflicting intuitions

Many different moral theories have been examined in this book. Each of these theories has something to recommend it, which explains why they all have competent contemporary advocates. However, each of them leads in some applications to difficulties. Conclusions can be drawn from each of them that seem to be at variance with some of our moral intuitions. No principled stance to ethical problems can find support among a *majority* when the trolley problems are discussed, for example. The egoist has a hard time explaining that we may do as we like in these cases, so long as we satisfy our own best interests. The utilitarian will have a hard time explaining that we are allowed to push the big man onto the track in the Footbridge case. The deontologists and the moral rights theorists must explain why it is wrong to divert the trolley to the loop where it will be stopped by running into a person tied to the track (who gets killed). The moral rights theorists have the additional problem of explaining that, if we so please, we need not do anything at all in the examples, thus allowing five innocent people to be killed. What conclusion should we draw from this? Should we conclude that we should avoid any principled stance to moral problems altogether and turn to virtue ethics or a feminist ethics of care?

No, not necessarily. For we should not accept just any intuition as a datum when we test a moral theory. We should test it against our own *considered* judgements rather than against mere in-tuitions. And we may have to revise our intuitions in order to arrive at a more coherent system of considered moral beliefs. Each person must do his best here. But this is not just a matter of creating a better coherence among one's exiting beliefs. We should also ponder the question: where do our intuitions come from?

Neuroscience and moral reasoning

Joshua D. Greene at Harvard University and his collaborators have studied extensively how we reach our verdicts in the trolley cases. Here are, in a very simplified form, some of their results about what happens when people react to the trolley cases. It seems as though a dual model makes best sense of us. On the one hand, controlled cognitive processes drive our utilitarian judgements, while non-utilitarian judgements (don't push the man) are driven by automatic, intuitive emotional responses. Different parts of our brains are responsible for these different responses, as can be seen from neuroimaging. 'Utilitarian' responses are associated with increased activity in the dorsolateral prefrontal cortex, a brain region associated with cognitive control (Greene et al., 'The Neural Bases of Cognitive Conflict and Control in Moral Judgment'). By cheering people up before we confront them with the examples it is possible to move them closer to the utilitarian camp (ibid.). By keeping people busy with intellectual tasks while giving their verdicts on the trolley cases, it is possible to move people closer to the non-utilitarian camp. Moreover, those who reach the utilitarian verdict have to overcome their own emotional resistance to the conclusion, which takes some time (ibid.). And people suffering from focal bilateral damage to the ventromedial prefrontal cortex, a brain region necessary for the normal generation of emotions and, in particular, social emotions, easily reach the utilitarian solution when asked about the cases (Koenigs et al., 'Damage to the Prefrontal Cortex Increases Utilitarian Moral Judgements').

When we know more about the origin of our moral intuitions, can this help us to select the right moral hypothesis, utilitarianism, the sanctity of life doctrine or some other doctrine? The results from neuroimaging of our brains and experimental psychological studies do not contradict our intuitions. They provide no evidence against them. But perhaps they can help us to undermine the *justification* for some of the intuitions in the same way that my knowledge that psychologists sometimes project holograms in front of me – in order to be able to mock me and my philosophy lectures where I claim to know that there is a table in front of me – would undermine my justification for my belief that there is a table in front of me.

Let us try this approach. Then which ones among the common intuitions to the trolley cases have their justification undermined by the scientific results showing us how they have come about?

This is a difficult question. It is obvious that some immediate intuitions among people at large just have to give way. You have to admit that, even if you are among the majority. You have to admit that, since there is *no* plausible theory consistent with *all* the intuitions. But if you want to get rid of some, but not all, of your intuitions, which ones should yield and which should be retained?

One could argue that we should try to muster the same emotional response to the Loop as the one we exhibit in relation to the Footbridge and opt for deontology (the sanctity of life doctrine). Or one could argue that our gut feelings, just because they are immediate and probably the result of a selective pressure way back in human history, lack credibility, and hence opt for the utilitarian solution.

There is something to each line of argument. However, the proper way of approaching our intuitions, it seems to me, is to see what our reactions to the examples are once we know about the origin of respective kinds of emotion. We should not rely on our intuitions before we know all that can be known about their origin. We should expose them to a kind of cognitive psychotherapy, then.

This is not enough, however. We need philosophical therapy as well. We must ascertain that we have correctly understood the examples. We are easily misguided when we ponder thought-examples. We read things into them that should not be there. The scientists who have studied our reactions have tried to compensate for this, but they may not have been entirely successful.

It is also important to make some distinctions, which are simply absent in the abstract description of the examples. We are here invited to assess what course of action is 'morally permissible'. It is not quite clear what this means. One question is what kind of response is right and what kind of response is wrong, when we abstract from long-term consequences (by assuming that there are no such consequences of importance). Another question is: what sort of people should we be – people who push, or people who don't push, the big man onto the track? A utilitarian may well admit that, in the long run, it is better that people at large are such that they don't push. And yet in the situation we ought to push. Some may be less willing to make this kind of distinction and claim that the crucial question is what sort of people we should be. But then they cannot respond to the trolley cases in a reasonable manner!

Philosophical subtleties like these are lost in the experiments. When they are added together with information about how our intuitions are formed, and comprehended, then, I submit, we are allowed to rely on the kind of (firm) intuitions we still hold. They are what I have called 'considered' intuitions. Our justification of them is not undermined by any knowledge we have been able to gain. Hence, quite reasonably, we take them to be indicative of the truth.

Inter-subjectivity

Can we expect inter-subjectivity in our thus considered moral intuitions? Perhaps, in the very long run, but even if there is room for hope, one cannot be sure about this. Ethics is different from science. Observations in science may be highly theory-laden and thus controversial, but there is always a possibility of moving to neutral ground when we account for them. One physicist may claim that he has observed a path of a positron in a cloud chamber. Another physicist claims that there is no such thing as a positron. He sees no trace of any positron. Now, there is a way of switching to a less theory-laden level of description of the content of their respective observations. Perhaps they can agree at least that there are certain traces of a certain shape, which they are watching. The physicist who believes he sees traces of a positron can urge the other scientist to explain what, if not traces of a positron passing, the traces they both see are traces *of*. However, in ethics there is no similar neutral ground, no clearly observable traces, to which we can move.

All this means, then, that different people may very well be justified in their beliefs in *competing* moral hypotheses. I may be justified in my belief in utilitarianism, while the Pope is justified in his belief in the sanctity of life doctrine, provided we have each scrutinised our intuitions properly. This may well be so; we may both be justified in our beliefs, but since utilitarianism and the

WHAT ARE WE TO BELIEVE?   139

sanctity of life doctrine contradict one another, they cannot both be true.

The possibility of such epistemic relativism may prompt us to believe that, after all, there is no truth in ethics. The idea that we should give up on some of our intuitions because they have been undermined by knowledge about their origin may come to be generalised to *all* our moral intuitions. We may be tempted to accept moral nihilism or moral relativism.

I think we ought to resist this temptation, but I must admit that, in the present context, I have not given any good argument to this effect. Let me just give one quotation from Derek Parfit, which strikes a similar optimistic chord:

> Disbelief in God, openly admitted by a majority, is a recent event, not yet completed. Because this event is so recent, Non-Religions Ethics is at a very early stage. We cannot yet predict whether, as in Mathematics, we will all reach agreement. Since we cannot know how Ethics will develop, it is not irrational to have high hopes. (*Reasons and Persons*, p. 454)

In the opening chapter I argued, also in the spirit of the quotation above, that God is irrelevant to normative ethics. One might have expected that the same is true of science. However, psychology and neural science seem to have a kind of indirect normative relevance, after all. We must consider scientific results when we try to find out whether our moral intuitions are reliable or not. By doing our best at arriving at well-considered moral intuitions – knowing how we have arrived at them, and by finding what are, in our own opinion, the best moral explanation of them – there is hope that we may end up in a reflective equilibrium where we are hence justified in our belief in one or another of the competing moral theories. However, even if we do, our acceptance of the theory must be somewhat preliminary and tentative. There is always the possibility that further thought about the principles, new experiences in our lives, new scientific results informing us about why we think and feel the way we do, or additional arguments, may bring about a change of opinion.

Why then strive so hard to arrive at a considered fundamental moral opinion if such an opinion is so difficult to come by? Why not rest satisfied with moral agnosticism?

But moral agnosticism is not a very substantial attitude to adopt. For it means that we have to solve hard practical questions without the guidance of a moral theory. We are left with a common-sense morality full of gaps, offering no advice in some situations where advice is most needed and leading to contradictory recommendations in other situations. Being a moral agnostic (with respect to basic moral principles) means also that we cannot learn in any systematic way from experience. If we do not hold on, at least tentatively, to some moral principles, we will never have any reason, in the light of new moral experience, to modify our views. If we have no basic moral principles, there is no way our basic moral outlook can be shown to be wanting. So the reason for forming a basic moral (principled) opinion, if only of a tentative nature, is that this is a way of growing morally more mature. By revising the basic view, when recalcitrant evidence emerges in the form of considered moral opinions at variance with conclusions drawn from the basic moral principle in a concrete case, we deepen our moral outlook. We revise our basic moral view, apply the new principle to the old case, in order to find a better moral explanation of it, but also to future cases ... until the time comes for a new revision. This seems to me to be the only responsible way of conducting moral thinking. To borrow a phrase from virtue ethics, a 'wise person' is characterised by such a moral outlook.

Is there a place for intellectual compromise?

All the theories reviewed in the book are, in some interpretation, inconsistent with each other. This means that a person who wants to avoid inconsistent beliefs cannot accept all of them. He or she can accept, at most, one of the conflicting theories. At least this is so if each theory is taken in an absolute form. However, why not try to revise and then combine them?

To some extent this may be a sound move. I have argued that the most plausible versions of virtue ethics and a feminist ethics of care do not present criteria of right action in competition with the other theories. If my argument is correct, then there is certainly room for some compromise here. The virtues are of importance no matter what basic moral principle we accept, and among them the tendency to care for others plays a crucial role.

However, the situation is different with the other theories. These theories are in competition with each other. This should not stop us from creating additional alternatives in this competition, of course, by constructing for ourselves combinations of restricted versions of the theories. I am thinking of combinations of the following kind. Why not in general maximise the sum total of welfare, but allow that, when the cost is too high for the agent, the agent pays special attention to his or her own interests? And why not add a clause from deontological ethics to the effect that even if maximisation of welfare is a perfectly reasonable end in most cases, this end does not justify means such as the deliberate killing of innocent human beings? As a matter of fact, this seems to be well in line with Kant's own view. And why not also add something from the theory of moral rights? Maximising the sum total of welfare is perfectly in order, but only to the extent that no moral rights are being violated. Or why not say that even if it is wrong to kill an innocent human being in order to save lives, if more than twenty-five innocent lives can be saved, it might be right to do so? Or, why not borrow from environmental ethics and say that it is perfectly permissible to foster human ends, but only to the extent that this does not mean that we degrade, spoil or destroy the natural environment? The list could easily be continued.

It must be left to the reader to think through combinations of the sort mentioned. However, it should not be taken for granted that such combinations of restricted versions of the theories will appear more plausible than the original ones, from which the combined parts were taken. A readiness for compromise may be a virtue in negotiations, where, in the final analysis, interests must be given their due weight. However, intellectual compromises often come at a high price. When the truth is sought, then the arguments count. And there is no weighing of arguments. An argument is either sound or it is flawed. So there is a definite risk that an intellectual compromise will import difficulties from each theory forming part of it without any gain in overall plausibility. Note that in morality, no less than in science, simplicity is an important virtue.

Let me add just one more warning against intellectual compromise. When such compromise is sought, there is a risk that the result will not only be complicated but indeterminate as well. We may end up with a moral system so loose that, in a particular case, when we want to turn to it for moral guidance, we find no help whatsoever. And this means that, once again, we are in the position of the moral agnostic. We cannot learn from our moral mistakes. If we cannot obtain any information from our moral system about what to do in specific situations, then we never run the risk of finding out (in a specific situation) that the information we obtain from our moral system is wrong. But this means that we are deprived of an important way of finding out if there is something wrong with our moral system. The system provides us with neither genuine moral explanation nor moral guidance. There is a risk, therefore, that if our system does not have any definite implications, we come to use it to rationalise all sorts of moral decisions. We use our moral system to hide our true reasons for action, both from ourselves and from others.

Moral particularism

I mentioned in Chapter 1 that I conceive of the search for a plausible moral principle as a search for the truth. This explains why there is a point in trying to eliminate inconsistencies in our moral thinking (two inconsistent beliefs cannot both be true). It also means that we are fallible in moral affairs (no matter how certain we are in a concrete case, or in our belief in a certain moral principle, we may be just plainly wrong about the moral realities). And I have indicated how one should go about in search of a plausible moral outlook. I also indicated why I do not think that moral relativism or nihilism poses any genuine threat to this kind of search. However, we have seen that some moral outlooks, such as virtue ethics and feminist ethics, do not share my enthusiasm for a principled approach to moral problems. We have already examined their respective reasons for a more in-direct approach. However, I should end this book by pointing out that there exists an even more radical opposition to the use of principles in moral philosophy, which has been called 'particularism'. According to particularism there is no point in the search for moral principles that can explain particular moral facts. And the reason why there is no point in the search for moral principles is very simple: there is no such thing as moral principles.

I have criticised particularism elsewhere. Here I will just note that with particularism goes a certain epistemological price. If we accept particularism, then we must give up one method of improving on our moral opinions and of gaining moral knowl-edge – the method used in this book. If moral particularism is true, then there is no way that we can make tentative moral explanations of particular cases in order to carry these tentative explanations (or putative moral principles) further to other cases in order to see whether they will or will not work in these other cases as well. According to particularism, what is a reason for a certain moral judgement in one situation may be no reason at all for the same judgement in another situation – it may even be a reason against the same judgement. But this means, it seems to me, that we should only take up particularism as our very last resort. We should not accept particularism before we have tried really hard to find plausible moral principles – and failed. So at least for a while, the business of normative ethics, as conceived of in this book, should go on.

Further reading about the role of principles in ethics

Much literature is forthcoming about the scientific studies about people dealing with trolley problems. Peter Singer argues in 'Ethics and Intuitions', *The Journal of Ethics*, vol. 9, 2005, pp. 331–52 that these studies not only undermine the anti-utilitarian intuitions, but also mean problems for the idea of a reflective equilibrium. His position is critically examined by Folke Tersman in 'The Reliability of Moral Intuitions: A Challenge from Neuroscience', *Australasian Journal of Philosophy*, vol. 86, 2008. In this chapter I have made references to Greene et al. (2004), 'The Neural Bases of Cognitive Conflict and Control in Moral Judgment', *Neuron*, vol. 44(2), 2004, pp. 389–400 and to M. Koenigs et al., 'Damage to the Prefrontal Cortex Increases Utilitarian Moral Judgements', *Nature*, 2007. An anthology with contributions sceptical of moral theory (moral principles) in ethics is Stanley G. Clarke and Evan Simpson (eds), *Anti-Theory in Ethics and Moral Conservatism* (Albany, NY: SUNY Press, 1989). An influential attack on the notion that ethics should be founded on explicit principles is Bernard Williams, *Ethics and the Limits of Philosophy* (London: Fontana, 1985). The most influential statement of particularism can be found in Jonathan Dancy, *Moral Reasons* (Oxford: Blackwell, 1993). I criticise particularism in Chapter 2 of my *Hedonistic Utilitarianism* (Edinburgh: Edinburgh University Press, 1998). For an attempted rebuttal of such arguments, see Brad Hooker and Margaret Olivia Little (eds), *Moral Particularism* (Oxford:

Clarendon Press, 2000), ch. 7. Particularism rejects moral principles altogether. It can be compared to a kind of deontology advocated by W. D. Ross (1877–1971). Ross too is sceptical about absolute moral principles, but he does not reject the notion as such of a moral principle. Ross put forward his theory about principles stating *prima facie* duties, rather than absolute ones, in *The Right and the Good* (Oxford: Clarendon Press, 1930).

Index

difference principle, 37, 39
diminishing marginal utility, 36, 37
Donagan, A., 72
Doris, J. M., 104
Dostoyevsky, F., 13
double effect (principle of), 62, 63,
    64, 67, 72
drugs as a means to mood enhance-
    ment, 24, 81

ecofeminism, 125
ecosystem, 124, 126
Edgeworth, F. Y., 28, 29
Eliot, R., 134
emotivism, 8, 16
euthanasia, 12, 61, 64, 65, 67, 69,
    70, 72, 79, 82, 87, 108
expected welfare (maximisation of),
    26, 27, 28, 30
experience machine (Nozick's), 23,
    24, 38
experience machine (used to measure
    pleasure), 28
expressivism, 16

Feldman, F., 38
Feminist Practical Discourse (FPD),
    118
Foole (Hobbes), the, 50, 51
Foot, P., 6, 16, 41, 61, 92, 101, 103,
    104, 106, 117
free will, 67, 71
free-riding, 49
Frey, R. G., 89
friendship, 22, 23, 25, 29, 30, 38, 40
future generations, 2, 52, 53

Gaia-hypothesis, 124, 128, 133
Gauthier, D., 51, 55
gene engineering, testing and therapy,
    3, 12, 127
generality, 43
generosity, 91
genetic test, 3
Gibbard, A., 16
Gilligan, C., 12, 109, 110, 111, 112,
    117, 118, 119
global warming, 2, 33, 44, 46, 120,
    123
Glover, J., 1, 16
God, 11, 12, 13, 14, 58, 77, 78, 125,
    126, 127, 139
good will, 52, 57, 97
Goslin, D. A., 118
Greene, J. D., 136, 143
Gregor, M., 72
Griffin, J., 38
Grotius, H., 76
guilt (moral), 66, 67, 68, 69

happiness, 18, 19, 21, 22, 38, 39, 42
Hare, R. M., 29
Harman, G., 16, 104, 134
Harris, J., 72
Harsanyi, J., 29
Hart, H. L. A., 133
heavy demands (the argument from),
    32, 38, 39, 41, 87
hedon (hedonistic atom), 29
hedonism, 18, 19, 20, 21 22, 23, 28,
    29, 32, 38, 39, 40, 121, 122,
    124, 128
hedonistic zero, 29
Held, V., 119
higher and lower pleasures, 21
Hinduism, 121
Hitler, A., 102
Hobbes, T., 12, 46, 47, 48, 49, 50,
    51, 52, 54, 74
Holy Scripture, 14
Hooker, B., 39, 143
Hume, D., 47, 54
Hursthouse, R., 93, 104
Hypatia, 105

imperfect (in contrast to strict,
    perfect) duty, 60
industry, 48, 91
infanticide, 88
innocent human being, 9, 11, 36, 57,
    60, 61, 64, 67, 69, 70, 72, 80,
    88, 135, 141
interpersonal comparisons of welfare,
    28, 29, 41
intrapersonal comparisons of welfare,
    29
intrinsic preferences, 22, 122
intrinsic value, 123, 129, 130, 131,
    133

Jaggar, A., 118, 119

psychological egoism, 47, 54
punishment, 49, 66, 67, 68, 69, 71,
    72, 83, 84, 85, 86, 96

Rachels, J., 72
Raiffa, H., 54
Rand, A., 42, 54
rationality, 42, 43
Rawls, J., 37, 39, 55, 100
reflective equilibrium, 10, 139, 143
Regan, T., 88, 89, 123
relativism (moral), 8, 16, 91, 139,
    142
repeated prisoner's dilemma, 48
repressive tolerance, 117
repugnant conclusion, 123, 133
Resnik, M. D., 54
Ross, W. D., 119, 133, 144
Rothbard, M. N., 89
Rousseau, J.-J., 107, 109, 115, 118,
    119
ruddy duck, 131, 132
rule utilitarianism, 39, 59, 60
Ryberg, J., 16, 133

sanctity of life doctrine, 61, 62, 64,
    65, 66, 67, 69, 70, 71, 72, 80,
    82, 84, 136, 137, 138, 139
Satan, 14, 127
scepticism (moral), 9
schizophrenia (moral), 31, 39
Schmidtz, D., 89
Scruton, R., 128
self-ownership, 73, 77
self-regarding preferences, 22
selling and buying of organs, 81
Shafer-Landau, R., 16
side-constraint, 73
Sidgwick, H., 30, 42, 54
simplicity, 43, 141
Simpson, E., 143
Singer, P., 16, 72, 122, 123, 133,
    143
Sir Peter Scott's Wildfowl Trust at
    Slimbridge, 132
Slatman, D., 104
Slote, M., 39, 93, 94, 95, 104, 113,
    114
Smart, J. J. C., 38

Socrates, 21, 106, 107
Sprigge, T., 128, 133
Stanford Encyclopedia of Philosophy,
    16, 133
state of nature, 48, 73
Steiner, H., 89
Stocker, M., 39
Sumner, L. W., 38, 89
survival lottery, 65, 66, 70, 72, 79,
    82, 87
suum, 76

Taylor, H., 17
Temkin, L. S., 39
temperance, 91, 106
Tersman, F., 143
the end justifies the means, 24, 34,
    82
Thomson, J. J., 6, 16, 41, 106, 117
tit-for-tat, 48, 49, 54
Tooley, M., 88
traffic regulation, 33
Tricky Dicky, 100
trolley cases, 6, 7, 16, 35, 39, 41, 42,
    61, 65, 80, 88, 97, 101, 105,
    117, 135, 136, 137, 138, 143
Tucker, A. W., 45
Tännsjö, T., 133

Unger, P., 31, 39
unit (hedonistic atom), 29

Vatican, the, 69, 72

Wallenberg, P., 81, 85
Warnock, M., 89
Westra, L., 134
white-hedded duck, 132
Williams, B., 32, 38, 143
wisdom (moral expertise), 91, 99,
    100, 103, 115, 117, 127
Wollstonecraft, M., 105, 107, 108,
    119
Woodward, P. A., 72

Young, I., 119

Zeno, 121
zero (hedonistic), 29